The Greek Americans

The
Greek
Americans

Other books in the
Immigrants in America series:

The
Greek
Americans

By Meg Greene

LUCENT BOOKS®

THOMSON
GALE

San Diego • Detroit • New York • San Francisco • Cleveland • New Haven, Conn. • Waterville, Maine • London • Munich

THOMSON

GALE

On cover: Easter candle lighting services at a Greek Orthodox Church.

LIBRARY OF CONGRESS CATALOGING-IN-PUBLICATION DATA

Greene, Meg.
  Greek Americans / by Meg Greene.
    v. cm. — (Immigrants in America)
Includes bibliographical references and index.
Contents: Introduction: The Greek odyssey — A country full of woe — "Mother I want
to go to foreign lands" — Coming to America — Ellis Island — The great adventure —
Living Greek, becoming American — Trying to fit.
  ISBN 1-59018-077-1 (hardback : alk. paper)
  1. Greek Americans—History—Juvenile literature. 2. Greek Americans—Social condi-
tions—Juvenile literature. 3. Immigrants—United States—History—Juvenile literature. 4.
Greece—Emigration and immigration—History—Juvenile literature. 5. United States—
Emigration and immigration—History—Juvenile literature. [1. Greek Americans. 2. Immigrants. 3. Greece—Emigration and immigration—History. 4. United States—Emigration and immigration—History.] I. Title. II. Series.
  E184.G7G75 2003
  973'.04893—dc21
                                      2003001225

Printed in the United States of America

CONTENTS

FOREWORD

Immigrants have come to America at different times, for different reasons, and from many different places. They leave their homelands to escape religious and political persecution, poverty, war, famine, and countless other hardships. The journey is rarely easy. Sometimes, it entails a long and hazardous ocean voyage. Other times, it follows a circuitous route through refugee camps and foreign countries. At the turn of the twentieth century, for instance, Italian peasants, fleeing poverty, boarded steamships bound for New York, Boston, and other eastern seaports. And during the 1970s and 1980s, Vietnamese men, women, and children, victims of a devastating war, began arriving at refugee camps in Arkansas, Pennsylvania, Florida, and California, en route to establishing new lives in the United States.

Whatever the circumstances surrounding their departure, the immigrants' journey is always made more difficult by the knowledge that they leave behind family, friends, and a familiar way of life. Despite this, immigrants continue to come to America because, for many, the United States represents something they could not find at home: freedom and opportunity for themselves and their children.

No matter what their reasons for emigrating, where they have come from, or when they left, once here, nearly all immigrants face considerable challenges in adapting and making the United States their new home. Language barriers, unfamiliar surroundings, and sometimes hostile neighbors make it difficult for immigrants to assimilate into American society. Some Vietnamese, for instance, could not read or write in their native tongue when they arrived in the United States. This heightened their struggle to communicate with employers who demanded they be literate in English, a language vastly different from their own. Likewise, Irish immigrant school children in Boston faced classmates who teased and belittled their lilting accent. Immigrants from Russia often felt isolated, having settled in areas of the United States where they had no access to traditional Russian foods. Similarly, Italian families, used to certain wines and spices, rarely shopped or traveled outside of New York's Little Italy, a self-contained community cut off from the rest of the city.

Even when first-generation immigrants do successfully settle into life in the United States, their children, born in America, often have different values and are influenced more by their country of birth than their parents' traditions. Children want to be a part of the American culture and usually welcome American ideals, beliefs, and styles. As they become more Americanized—adopting western dating habits and fashions, for instance—they tend to cast aside or even actively reject the traditions embraced by their parents. Assimilation, then, often becomes an ideological dispute that creates conflict among immigrants of every ethnicity. Whether Chinese, Italian, Russian, or Vietnamese, young people battle their elders for respect, individuality, and freedom, issues that often would not have come up in their homeland. And no matter how tightly the first generations hold onto their traditions, in the end, it is usually the young people who decide what to keep and what to discard.

The Immigrants in America series fully examines the immigrant experience. Each book in the series discusses why the immigrants left their homeland, what the journey to America was like, what they experienced when they arrived, and the challenges of assimilation. Each volume includes discussion of triumph and tragedy, contributions and influences, history and the future. Fully documented primary and secondary source quotations enliven the text. Sidebars highlight interesting events and personalities. Annotated bibliographies offer ideas for additional research. Each book in this dynamic series provides students with a wealth of information as well as launching points for further discussion.

INTRODUCTION

The Greek Odyssey

In 1913, the world of a man named Michael Pappas changed dramatically. Born a Greek in Turkish-occupied territory, Pappas faced an uncertain future. Like thousands of other Europeans, he had made the difficult decision to go to America. Years later, when asked why he had chosen to leave his home and come to the United States, Pappas replied "Greece was poor—I had no future there. It was better to go to New York which was in those days, like we know, the richest country in the world, with more chances, more future. I was only sixteen. That's why I decided to come to America."[1] Although Pappas's early years in America proved lonely and difficult, he gradually overcame the hardships and built a successful restaurant, acquired a 105-acre farm, and had a winter home in Florida. If he had stayed in Greece, his life almost surely would have been much different.

Opening the Gate

Michael Pappas was one of the approximately 370,000 Greek immigrants who came to the United States between 1890 and 1920. The Greeks were just one of many peoples from southern and eastern Europe who crowded their way onto the ships bound for America and filed through the gates of Ellis Island, one of the primary ports of entry into the United States. All came in search of a new life. But for the Greeks who came, there would be a continual tension between their new homeland and the one they had left behind; as they are a proud people who remain passionate in their devotion to their ancestral homeland and to their culture.

Throughout history, it has been the sad fate of Greece to become embroiled in conflicts with its neighbors and, at times, with itself. The constant threat of war and the continual internal unrest and economic turmoil that dominated the late nineteenth and earlier twentieth centuries persuaded many Greeks to look to the United States as a refuge and a chance to start life anew. The majority of these immigrants were like Michael Pappas: young men who had no money and few, if any, skills. They had ventured to America in search of work, but many planned on returning home as soon as they had made their fortune. The pull of Greece was very powerful. Yet, America was their dream. It offered the prospect of opportunity, wealth, and, perhaps most important, a chance to become a success.

Like most immigrants to the United States in the early twentieth century, this Greek family enters the country through Ellis Island.

A Strong Presence

Although the years 1890 to 1920 marked the largest and most sustained period of Greek immigration, the Greeks have had an important presence in the United States for more than two hundred years. Early figures are hard to calculate, for the American Immigration Service did not make the first reference to Greeks until 1824. During the first half of the nineteenth century, Greek immigration evidently proceeded slowly. Records indicate that in 1848 one Greek arrived in the United States compared with 91,061 Irish and 51,593 German immigrants. In 1850, the official Greek immigration figure doubled when two Greeks arrived.

In reality, small numbers of Greeks had steadily come to the United States throughout the early nineteenth century. Many of them were sailors who arrived in port cities and stayed to work for American shipping companies on the Mississippi River and the Great Lakes. Some Greeks became cotton brokers or merchants in the South, while others established thriving import-export businesses in New York, Boston, San Francisco, and New Orleans. The willingness of Greek immigrants to work hard produced numerous success stories that seemed to represent the fulfillment of the American dream in which one acquires money, property, and success.

During the 1890s, the first great wave of Greek immigration began. Thousands of Greeks entered Ellis Island in New York City to escape the crushing poverty and the ongoing political crises in their country. The number of Greeks arriving was substantial and continued to flow for well over thirty years.

With the passage of the Immigration Act of 1924, which severely restricted the number of people permitted to enter the country from southern and eastern Europe, the first wave of Greek immigration came to an end. By 1930, the number of Greek immigrants allowed into the United States had dropped by more than half.

The number of Greek immigration to the United States remained low for approximately twenty-five years, with an annual average of between 3,000 and 4,000. At the end of the Second World War in 1945, however, Greece plunged into a civil war between partisans and Communists. From 1947 until 1949, thousands of Greeks left to come to the United States to escape the horrors of the war that ravaged their country. In the mid-1950s, the number of Greek immigrants steadily rose, as many Greeks sought refugee status under the Refugee Relief Act. This act, passed by Congress in 1953, allowed displaced persons, or those who had no homes in their native country, to emigrate in the United States.

Greek America

According to the 2000 census, approximately 1,179,000 Greeks and people of Greek ancestry reside in the United States. Various Greek American organizations, however, maintain that there are, in fact, closer to 3 million people of Greek descent living in America, making up the largest community of Greeks in the world outside Greece itself, and one of the largest immigrant groups in the United States. Greek Americans live in every state, though the majority can be found in the Northeast and

The United States Supreme Court in Washington, D.C., is modeled after classical Greek architecture. Greek traditions have influenced many facets of American life.

the Midwest. The single largest Greek American neighborhood is located in Astoria, in the borough of Queens in New York City. Approximately 35,000 Greek Americans live there. Philadelphia, Boston, Chicago, St. Louis, and San Francisco also have large Greek American communities.

Greek Americans have made many valuable contributions to American society and life. Since their arrival in the United States, Greeks have enriched their adopted land with their customs, culture, institutions, and cuisine. While early Greek immigrants worked hard to establish a place for themselves and their families in mainstream American society, more recent immigrants and second- and third-generation Greek Americans now face the challenge of balancing their American identity and their Greek heritage. Their efforts to do so serve to remind them of their forebearers, who made their way to American shores more than a century before.

CHAPTER ONE

A Country Full of Woe

The flood of Greek immigrants who came to the United States during the late nineteenth and early twentieth centuries left behind a land deeply engulfed in strife. By the 1890s Greece had a population of approximately 2.5 million people, making it an overcrowded region where land was becoming increasingly scarce. Also in short supply was economic prosperity, as many Greeks struggled to make a living. With the exception of the major port cities, large areas of Greece remained mired in poverty, with people living much as their forebearers had done generations ago.

Greeks have always admired the natural beauty of their country and savored its rich traditions and glorious history, yet rather than dwelling on the past, Greeks have sought to modernize. Hoping that the introduction of new technologies would bring greater economic prosperity, Greece was eager to compete with other nations. These efforts at best met with incomplete success and thus did little to dissuade Greeks from leaving to seek their fortunes abroad.

A New Prosperity

A visitor to Greece in 1895 would have seen a country in the midst of change, a complex mixture of old and new, ancient and modern. In Athens, the capital, home to the ancient philosophers Socrates and Plato, and birthplace of democracy, business was booming, with factories in operation around the clock. Here, and in other Greek cities, new skyscrapers dwarfed temples thousands of years old. Men and women who had lived all their lives in the Greek countryside scrambled to the cities in search of work. Even with this influx, there was a shortage of skilled laborers such as masons, carpenters, and plasterers. Given the hustle and bustle of the cities, it seemed as if all of Greece was prosperous and thriving.

Greece also boasted a growing merchant fleet that ranked fourth in size in the world, behind that of Great Britain, Norway, and Denmark. By the end of the nineteenth century, Piraeus was the third-largest port city on the Mediterranean, trailing only Marseilles in southern France and Genoa in northern Italy. Domestic and foreign investment increased the number of vessels in the Greek fleet from 107 to 201, with net tonnage growing from 86,968 tons to 214,814 tons.

Looking to the Future

Adding to the growing prosperity of Greece was the large sum of foreign capital pouring into the country. Bankers and merchants in many western European countries, such as France, Germany, and Belgium, were attracted to the potential profits to be made by investing in Greek mines, banks, businesses, and the newly created Greek utilities industry, symbolized by the highly successful Greek Electric Company, which provided electricity to Athens and its environs.

In addition, investors put their money into the construction of a new electric rail-way that promised to create more businesses, profits, and jobs. At the same time, other new rail lines were being built in southwestern Greece, linking the farmers of this region to urban markets. Meanwhile, completion of the Corinth Canal in 1893 was crucial to the continued economic health of Greece. The canal, which linked the Isthmus of Corinth to the Saronic Gulf, shortened the journey from the Adriatic Sea to the port cities of Austria, Italy, and France in the west and those of Turkey, Russia, and Asia to the east.

Completed in 1893, the Corinth Canal contributed to Greece's economic prosperity.

Nothing, then, appeared able to stop the rising tide of Greek prosperity. A severe drought brought massive crop failures in 1899, however, and a decline in the value of the drachma, the basic unit of Greek currency, threatened to undo the prosperity of the previous decade. Fortunately, this economic downturn did not last long, and soon the country had resumed its affluent course. Greece seemed to be on the threshold of a new and prosperous era in its already long and glorious history. It was not to be. While the manufacturing and commercial cities enjoyed riches, the rural areas, in which the vast majority of Greeks still lived, endured poverty and deprivation.

The Limits of Prosperity

According to Theodore Saloutos, a historian of Greek immigration, to understand Greece of the late nineteenth century "one must know the rural areas, the villages and the peasants, more so than the cities, ports, banks, railroads, and public improvements."[2] During this period, the majority of the Greek people lived in the countryside and made their living by farming. There were also a number of small manufacturers, merchants, and tradesmen who primarily served the agricultural economy, as well as workers in the growing transportation industry, and civil servants employed in the provincial governments.

Even in the best of times, life in the rural villages could be hard; many residents lived in relentless poverty. Dry and rocky, the land was inhospitable to farming. Starvation was a fact of life; famine a constant threat. The prosperity that flourished in the cities was nowhere in evidence here. In a magazine interview that he gave after coming to America, a Greek immigrant described life in a rural village:

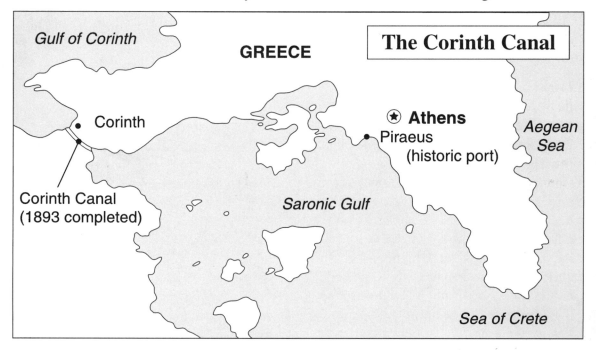

Gulf of Corinth

GREECE

The Corinth Canal

• Corinth

⭐ **Athens**
Piraeus
(historic port)

Aegean Sea

Corinth Canal
(1893 completed)

Saronic Gulf

Sea of Crete

A woman gathers water from a communal fountain in a village near Corinth. Life in rural villages in Greece was very difficult.

I was born about forty years ago in a little hamlet among the mountains of Laconia in Greece. There were only about 200 people in this place, and they lived in stone huts or cottages, some which were two stories high, but most of them only one story. The people were shepherds or small farmers. . . . As a general rule, when we wanted to buy anything we had to go down to Sparta, the chief town of our State, which was two hours' walk away from our village. . . . [The people] made almost everything for themselves. The inside of [a] cottage consisted of one large room with a board floor. . . . The fireplace at one end of the room was large and open; beds were made of boards covered with hay. . . . Cooking was done on an iron tripod with the fire underneath. . . . We had very little money, and so little use for money that the currency might almost as well have been the iron sort of our remote forefathers.[3]

One of the biggest reasons for the poverty was the failure of the peasants to acquire land. Estimates suggest that among 120,000

Hoping to find work, rural Greeks crowd the streets of Athens.

farm families in Greece in 1833, only 20,000, or only one family out of every six, owned the land they worked. Although landownership was the dream of many Greek peasants, the government unfortunately seemed indifferent to their needs.

Instead of selling the land to Greek farmers, the government instead chose to keep it. As a result, by 1842 approximately two-thirds (67 percent) of the country's estimated 5 million acres of farmland was idle. Selling the land to the peasants not only would have given them some hope of escaping poverty, but also undoubtedly would have eased the crush of people crowded onto available land and provided additional revenue for the government in the form of property taxes. Government

officials, however, thought differently and preferred to remain "land rich," believing that land was the one asset that would retain its value. Many peasants tried to save to buy what land was available for purchase, but they earned so little that it was virtually impossible to accumulate enough for a down payment. Others tried to borrow money, but astronomical interest rates ranging between 70 and 80 percent, undermined their plans.

Too Many People

The shortage of available land also affected the population of Greece. During the late nineteenth and early twentieth centuries, the population grew at a rapid rate, causing massive overcrowding throughout the country. Hardest hit were the rural areas, in which there was already a shortage of farmland.

By 1931, Greece averaged 870 inhabitants per square mile of cultivated land; for comparison, in the United States at that time there were 41.2 persons per square mile. The population grew steadily, and by the middle of the twentieth century, births exceeded deaths by a ratio of 2 to 1. The population boom, along with a shortage of land, put a tremendous strain on Greek society. People could not acquire land to farm and, because the population had grown so rapidly, it became more difficult for them to find work. The abundance of potential workers and the competition for jobs also depressed wages for those fortunate enough to find employment. The result was that many men and women were out of work and unable to find any means of making a living.

Taxes, Taxes, and More Taxes

The system of taxes compounded the peasants' economic and financial woes. The fiscal policies of the Greek government favored the cities. By the late nineteenth century, the government had spent lavishly to finance the construction of impressive public buildings, improved transportation systems, utilities, and port facilities, all for the cities. By contrast, the government neglected improvements that would have aided the peasants, such as draining marshes, building irrigation canals, or repairing roads. Politicians remained largely indifferent to the welfare of rural Greeks, who lacked the political clout of urban residents. Few government officials even bothered to visit the countryside to see firsthand the problems people faced. This evident neglect raised tensions between the countryside and the city—tensions that Saloutos thought originated in "the arrogance of the educated and privileged minorities of the cities toward the ignorant, downtrodden and neglected peasantry."[4]

To add insult to injury, the government imposed higher taxes on the small farmers and peasants to help pay for improvements that benefited the cities. Many rural Greek peasants strongly resented a government that they believed ignored and neglected them and then expected them to bear the brunt of a tax burden that consumed between 10 and 40 percent of their already meager incomes. By comparison, the government taxed small companies at a rate of only 5 percent, while the members of the ruling class paid nothing. The obvious injustice of the situation prompted one Greek immigrant to exclaim that the peasants paid "taxes on taxes without seeing any improvement."[5]

Greek peasants who could not afford to pay taxes in cash were allowed to pay them in kind, that is, by turning over to the government a portion of their crop. Yet, here, too, problems arose. The government required one-tenth of the crop as payment. In a fertile year, that condition was fairly easy and painless to meet. Yet, in bad years, the government did not adjust its rates. The peasant farmers still had to pay 10 percent. Moreover, the tax collectors took the finest

In Search of a Better Life

Although the overwhelming majority of people worked the land, agricultural work held a fairly low status in Greek society. For this reason, many Greek parents pushed their sons toward other professions such as the law or medicine, positions that were financially more secure and were held in higher regard in Greek society. There was also a shortage of lawyers and doctors. In 1907, for example, there was only one lawyer for every 828 persons in Greece and one doctor for every 888 persons. Still, for many years, the majority of Greeks (at one time almost 67 percent of the entire population) were still living in rural areas and engaged in some form of farm work.

produce, leaving Greek farmers little incentive to produce a hardy and healthy crop, since they knew the government would confiscate the best they had raised for taxes.

Although the government supervised tax collection, the actual process was in the hands of private contractors who routinely abused their authority. The collector set the day for the tax collection and did not always take into account whether the crop was ready for harvest. Some farmers had to transport their crops for miles to the place where taxes were being collected. Many complained about the taxes they paid and the manner of their collection, but cries for reform went unheeded.

As a result, peasants sometimes took matters into their own hands. They threatened violence against tax assessors and tax collectors, and many simply refused to pay. These actions had an effect on government revenues: Between 1882 and 1891, the Greek national treasury held only 75,278,420 drachmas, which is approximately $4,262,154 in current U.S. dollars. Even as Greece seemed to be enjoying unprecedented affluence, the state itself teetered on the edge of bankruptcy, stumbling toward financial collapse.

A Nation in Turmoil

Greece also had more than its share of political problems. For more than two thousand years, Greece had been under the control of one foreign power after another. Finally, in 1829, the Greeks fought for and won their independence from the Ottoman Turks. In the years following independence,

however, the Greek government continued to struggle.

Within a few years of independence, the Greek government, which had been a monarchy, was challenged by an oligarchy, a government dominated by a few very influential people. This ruling group immediately set about to limit the powers of King Otto I, who reigned from 1832 to 1862. The tension between the Greek monarchy and the ambitious oligarchy began in 1833, the year after Otto I ascended to the throne. Yet, despite the efforts of the oligarchy to take control of the government, Otto initially managed to consolidate his power, and Greece was once more ruled as a monarchy. Early success, however, did not end his problems, for he remained unpopular throughout his reign. Otto was not Greek. He was German. His full name was Otto Friedrich Ludwig. The London Conference of 1832, which took place to settle the outstanding issues that remained from the Greek war against Turkey, had appointed Otto to rule an independent Greece. The Greeks, unsurprisingly, did not wish to be governed by a foreigner. In addition, Otto was not a member of the Greek Orthodox Church, the majority religion in Greece. His imposition of high taxes and his use of German officials in key positions in the government added to his growing unpopularity. In 1843 an insurrection forced him to grant a constitution that somewhat restricted his power. Nineteen years later, in 1862, a coup removed him from the throne.

In 1863 the Greek National Assembly elected George I as king, and he reigned until his death in 1913. The second son of King Christian IX of Denmark, George en-

The Dowry

Some Greek women were forced to emigrate as the result of a centuries-old custom: the dowry. According to this tradition, a bride's family was obliged to provide her future husband with a dowry or offering, which was often money, livestock, or land. As a result, fathers and brothers often worked very hard to make sure that the female members of the family had these dowries. Without them, a woman had more difficult odds of being married. To provide dowries for their female relatives, some men emigrated to America. Some women, who were unable to secure dowries, also left Greece in the hopes of eventually finding a husband in America. But generally, most women preferred to stay in Greece, believing that the men who had gone to America to make their fortunes would one day return.

joyed better relations with the oligarchy even though he, like Otto, was neither Greek nor Orthodox. Working closely with members of the oligarchy, for example, George I blocked the efforts of Prime Minister Harilaos Trikoupis to make the national government more democratic. Limiting the spread of democracy in Greece enabled the king and the members of the oligarchy, many of whom George had appointed to important offices, to control almost all aspects of Greek political, economic, diplomatic, and military life.

Under the rule of George I, the lower classes still had to shoulder a heavy tax burden, just as they had had to do under Otto. Equally galling was the policy of compulsory military service for all able-bodied men over the age of nineteen. Increasing numbers of men were affected as George I became more ambitious to acquire territory, particularly land held by Greece's age-old enemy, Turkey. In 1881 George incorporated parts of Thessaly and Epirus into his realm, and in 1896–1897 he again used the military to put down an insurrection on the island of Crete. Greece also joined Bulgaria, Montenegro, and Serbia to defeat Turkey in the First Balkan War of 1912–1913. Few ordinary soldiers shared in the glory of these victories, however, for life in the military was hard. Harsh discipline, poor pay (in many cases consisting of one cigarette a day), faulty equipment, shabby uniforms, and inadequate and often tainted food made the life of the average soldier miserable.

Caught Between Two Countries

For Greeks living in Turkish-occupied territory that had once belonged to Greece, life was even grimmer. These Greeks were subject to Turkish law that did not treat them as the equals of the Turks themselves. In addition, hostilities between Turkey and Greece in the early twentieth century prompted the Turks to look upon the Greeks in their midst with even greater

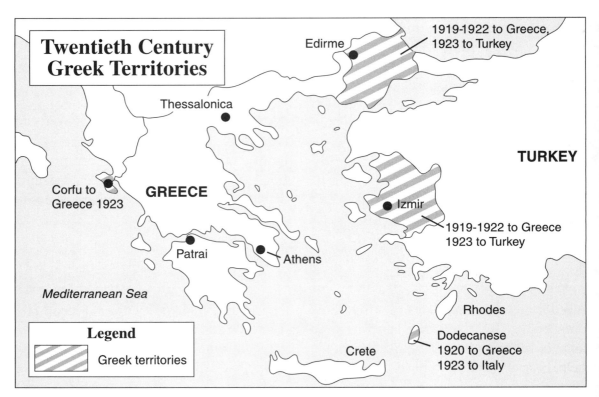

Twentieth Century Greek Territories

1919-1922 to Greece, 1923 to Turkey

Edirme

Thessalonica

TURKEY

Corfu to Greece 1923

GREECE

Izmir

1919-1922 to Greece 1923 to Turkey

Patrai

Athens

Mediterranean Sea

Legend

Greek territories

Rhodes

Dodecanese 1920 to Greece 1923 to Italy

Crete

suspicion. When the First Balkan War broke out in 1912, James Karavolas, who later immigrated to the United States, remembered that his family was caught between two armies. After his village was bombed, Karavolas recalled walking through the streets with his father and seeing bodies piled on the sidewalk. The bombs had left huge craters in the streets, and blood was everywhere. Standing in the street, Karavolas's father made the decision to sell everything he had to get his family out of Greece.

More Troubled Times

Throughout the twentieth century, Greece continued to be plagued by conflict and dissent. As a result, whenever possible, Greeks continued to leave for the United States. In 1913 the country was again plunged into crisis with the assassination of King George I at Salonika. His death brought his son Constantine to the throne. Constantine, who ruled Greece from 1913 to 1917 and again from 1920 to 1922, favored neutrality in the First World War. However, the Allied powers of France, Great Britain, Italy, and the United States, with the help of Eleuthérios Venizélos, the former premier of Greece, forced Constantine to give up the throne in 1917 in favor of his son Alexander. Greece soon thereafter entered the war in support of the Allies. Allied victory in 1918 enabled Greece to recover some of its former territory, which Turkey, an ally of Germany, had held.

Still hostilities with Turkey did not cease. In 1921 Greece again attacked Turkey, but this time suffered a humiliating defeat at

Anatolia. A peace treaty returned control of Greek territory to Turkey, including Greek-occupied lands in Asia Minor. The disaster again forced Constantine, whom a popular vote had restored to the throne in 1920, to abdicate, this time in favor of his son George.

George II, who sat on the throne for only one year, did not fare well. Just as immigration restrictions were being put in place in the United States, the Greek army invaded Asia Minor to regain lost territory and suffered another terrible defeat at the port city of Smyrna. Turkish soldiers went on a killing and looting frenzy, slaughtering innocent Greeks and Armenians. The number of casualties ran into the thousands, as people tried to reach nearby ships for help. Fearing Turkish reprisals, many of the ships refused to take on refugees. One refugee later recalled the horror of that time: "Many people were left behind . . . they hoped to get on the ships but they never did because the Turks had them completely surrounded and none could get away."[6] It was only because of ships owned by Britons and Greeks that 125,000 refugees were saved. But the defeat also left behind 1.3 million Greek refugees. Many were sent to Greece but had difficulty adjusting, for having lived in Turkish-occupied lands, they spoke only Turkish. To them, their historic homeland was really a foreign place. Greeks in name only, they looked elsewhere, to Europe and America, to make a new home.

Finally, less than a year after coming to power, George II abandoned the throne in 1923. But instead of forming a constitutional government to replace the king, General Theodoros Panga declared himself dictator in 1926. By the following year, however, he was forced from power and imprisoned. A period of relative peace and stability now settled over the country. George II returned to the throne in 1935 as the result of a popular vote. Yet, he was a king without authority, as another powerful government official, General Ionnis Metaxas, became dictator in 1936. This continual instability within the Greek government pushed many people to leave the country.

A New Enemy, Then Chaos

In 1940 Greece came under attack from a new enemy. During the Second World War, the Italian army invaded Greece but was driven back by stubborn Greek Resistance fighters. To aid their Italian allies, the Nazis invaded and occupied Greece. With the Nazi invasion, Greece experienced devastating destruction as troops looted villages and cities, took away needed animals for their own use, and confiscated crops. People died from hunger and disease. George II and the rest of the Greek government fled into exile, first to Crete, then to England, and finally to Cairo. The Germans withdrew from Greece in 1944, but it was not until 1946 that the king and the government returned.

With the Nazis defeated and the Second World War at an end, Greece faced yet another serious problem when a group of Greek Communists, who had earlier fought with the Resistance against German troops, refused to disband their forces. As a consequence, a civil war broke out in Greece between Communist insurgents and Greek

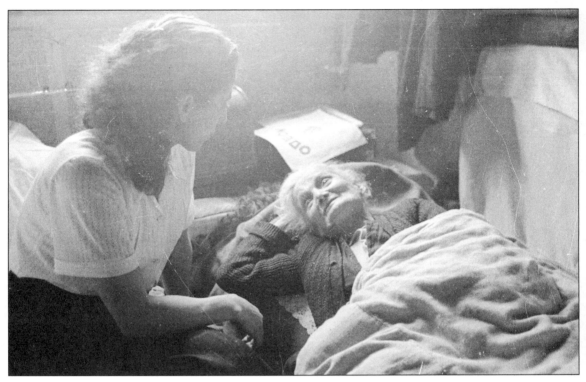

An elderly Greek woman is comforted by her daughter. During her lifetime, Greece was in an almost constant state of war.

loyalists, which with great difficulty the British at last managed to suppress. Yet, the Communists remained powerful enough to control most of the country outside Athens and Thessaloníki. Even though the Communists accepted the restoration of democratic government and the return of the king in 1946, they also revived a civil war that did not end until 1949. During this period the Communists formed a provisional government in the mountains of northern Greece but were ultimately defeated with aid from the United States.

With help from the United States, Greece recovered from the immediate consequences of civil war, but a series of unstable governments slowed the process of reconstruction and left the Greek people feeling even more demoralized and destitute. By the early 1950s, many Greeks were taking advantage of the loosening immigration restrictions and coming to America.

Further cause to leave came in April 1967 when a group of army officers, known as "the colonels," seized power in the name of the king, though the monarch himself was not involved in the coup and later fled the country. The new military rulers imposed strict censorship, banned labor strikes and public meetings, and imprisoned, tortured, and killed anyone who spoke out against them. In 1973 the military regime abolished the monarchy and declared Greece a republic. Bloody riots broke out in Athens as left-wing students challenged the government. In the chaos that followed, Brigadier

General Dimitrios Ioannidis led a coup against the government and seized power, returning Greece to democratic rule in 1974. But that did not stop thousands of Greeks, many of them professionals and students, from leaving the country. George Kokkas, along with thousands of his countrymen, left Greece to escape the bloodshed and political oppression. In an interview he stated that "the war in 1967 was very bad. The political system in Greece—the king and the prime ministers fought each other, so they didn't take care of the people, only of themselves."[7] Kokkas and countless other Greeks believed that there must be a better way to live, even if they had to leave their homeland to find it.

It seemed then, that for well over seventy-five years, life continued to be hard and uncertain for many Greeks. Even though the country did enjoy some periods of prosperity and political calm, they were too fleeting. To escape unemployment, poverty, oppressive taxation, and obligatory military service, many Greeks began to consider leaving their homeland for what they hoped would be a better, safer, and happier life abroad.

CHAPTER TWO

"Mother, I Want to Go to Foreign Lands"

During the late nineteenth century, Greece was beset by economic hardship, political turbulence, and social instability. The growing economic problems found many Greeks struggling to overcome terrible poverty. Most failed. Agriculture, still the basis of the Greek economy, was primitive, and key cash crops such as olives and currants were no longer in worldwide demand, plunging Greece further into economic distress. The great push for modernization was confined to the cities, and needed improvements for the rural areas, such as the construction of roads and irrigation systems, were not forthcoming.

For many Greeks, the situation had become intolerable. They realized that change, if it occurred at all, would be a long time coming. Many now seriously considered immigration. As difficult as it would be to leave behind family, friends, and all that was familiar, many thought that they had no choice. There were few opportunities for them to have a better life in Greece. Perhaps they should look across the sea for a second chance at success. For thousands, the United States of America became the land in which they could realize their dreams.

Why America?

The image of America as a land of "golden opportunities" was a powerful draw for immigrants from all over the world. Even though many knew only vaguely where the United States was located, people often had clear expectations of what they would find once they got there. For some, it was a place where their children might receive an education; others were responding to the lure of becoming rich. For those fleeing religious persecution or political unrest, America with its democratic government and policy of religious tolerance seemed almost too good to be true. Bessie Spylios, who traveled with her family in 1909 to America remembers her first impressions:

"Everybody was saying it was a land to make money, to have freedom, to do whatever you please." [8]

One important event helped encourage the mass migrations to the United States: the Industrial Revolution. Beginning in Britain during the eighteenth century, the Industrial Revolution then spread to western Europe and the United States. New technology making use of steam and water, as well as the discovery of new materials, helped boost manufacturing and increase production. The growth of factories

Greek farmers travel to market with their produce. Greeks came to America in search of greater opportunity.

A Cash Crop Becomes a Liability

Many Greeks left their country during the 1890s as the result of a decline in the price of currants, a kind of raisin, which had once been a booming cash crop. France and Russia, which had had setbacks with their currant vineyards, were two of Greece's biggest customers. France alone purchased more than half of the annual currant crop, which amounted to between sixty and seventy thousand tons a year. But when French vineyards regained their productive capacity, there was no longer a need to purchase Greek currants. Also the French and Russians passed protective tariffs that virtually outlawed the shipment of Greek currants to their countries. The sharp decline in prices was a severe blow to the Greek economy. Also adding to the farmers' problems was the decision of many to destroy their olive groves to plant the more profitable currant crop. The response of many Greeks to this downturn was simply to leave.

in the United States spurred a need for cheap labor, most of which was provided by immigrants coming in search of jobs.

The Greeks and others who emigrated to the United States during the late nineteenth and early twentieth centuries also took advantage of the great advances that had been made in transportation. Major improvements in rail and transatlantic travel now made it easier than ever for people to move from country to country and even overseas. As a result, the Industrial Revolution, with its impact on business, manufacturing, and travel, helped influence a change in the social and economic life of people in Europe and the United States by determining not only how people would earn a living, but where they would live and how they would move.

But perhaps more important than cheap transportation or plentiful jobs was the opportunity for many immigrants to change the course of their lives. In Europe, a person's destiny was shaped by how much money or land he or she had inherited, or even where the person was born. America offered the chance to break out of the cycle of poverty.

The Forging of Bonds

Historically, relations between the United States and Greece had been more philosophical than actual. After the American Revolution, for instance, when American statesmen pondered the creation of a new government, they looked to the republican city-states of ancient Greece, especially Athens, as one model to guide their efforts. For much of its history, Athens had been a democracy, a government of the people by the people. Rather than reestablishing a monarchy or granting power to a small ruling elite, the founding fathers drew on the Athenian democratic ideal and put more political power into the hands of the citizens.

Throughout the nineteenth century, democracy in America became more widespread and involved growing numbers of Americans.

Recognizing the Greek origins of democratic government, many Americans supported the Greek fight for independence during the 1820s. They viewed the struggle against the Ottoman Empire as similar to their own revolution against Great Britain. To aid the Greek patriots, Americans formed so-called relief committees, and the president of the United States, John Quincy Adams, spoke out publicly in favor of the Greek cause. Champions of Greek independence became known as "philhellenes," or "lovers of Greece and things Greek." Some Americans even went to Greece to help fight against the Turks. Greek children, orphaned by the war, were brought to the United States to be adopted and raised by American families.

By the late nineteenth century, American relations with Greece had become more tangible. The United States formed commercial ties with Greece. Trade between the two countries consisted mostly of black olives and Peloponnesian root, an herb used for cooking and medicinal purposes. American merchants, though, wished to do even more business with Greece. Many companies learned that the Greeks who could afford the expense preferred to buy American-made watches, sewing machines, and other manufactured goods instead of products made in Europe, because the U.S. goods were often of better quality. Some American businessmen were so enthusiastic about the possibility of opening new markets in Greece that they flooded the Greek mail with catalogs and other advertisements, not realizing that few Greeks could read English.

"To Foreign Lands I Must Go"

The notion of moving to a better place was nothing new to the Greeks. Since the earliest days of the Greek empire, Greeks had proved themselves curious and enterprising adventurers and businessmen. The lyrics of a popular folk song summed up the Greek wanderlust: "Mother, I want to go to foreign lands. To foreign lands I must go."[9]

During the 1880s and the 1890s, it was becoming clear to many Greeks that they would never escape the poverty that engulfed their homeland, especially in the rural, agricultural districts. Some saw the possibility of earning a better living in the United States and of giving themselves and their children a better life. Fathers and sons wanted to provide daughters or sisters with a suitable dowry so that they might marry well. Others, tired of farming, wanted to experience life in an American city. Once the mass exodus of Greek men began, many a Greek woman also wished to come to America to find a husband.

Greeks living in Turkish-occupied lands also saw opportunities in the United States. For many years, they had enjoyed a relatively peaceful and secure existence under Turkish rule. However, by the early twentieth century, the new Turkish government did not view the Greeks in the same benevolent light as had the earlier Ottoman rulers. Realizing that economic opportunities, and perhaps individual security, were now uncertain if they remained in Turkey, many

Greeks opted to go to America. The economic hardships and political tumult of their own country prevented them from returning to Greece. The United States seemed the one place on Earth where they could attain freedom, make a decent living, and perhaps, if they were hardworking and fortunate, strike it rich.

The "Brain Drain"

B ecause immigration to the United States is easier now than in the years between 1924 and 1945, many highly qualified Greeks have come to America in search of better job and educational opportunities. Between 1957 and 1961, Greece lost over one-fifth of its engineering graduates to the United States. During the years from 1962 to 1969, 586 engineers, 271 scientists, and 209 physicians and surgeons left Greece. Because this group tends to be financially better off and better educated than the first waves of Greek immigrants, the Greek government became concerned over the "brain drain." With more professionals leaving, a shortage of doctors, lawyers, college instructors, and engineers began to be noticed in the country. To offset this, in 1974 an association of Greek American scientists, engineers, educators, and other professionals formed "Krikos." The goal of the organization is to reverse "brain drain" by applying their expertise to help Greece develop more fully.

The Lure of Opportunity

It seemed as if everywhere the Greeks turned, moneylenders, steamship lines, and even their own government described the great fortunes to be made in America. Circulars, pamphlets, and newspaper advertisements placed by American businesses, steamship lines, and in some cases Greek immigrants already in America asked Greeks why they continued to struggle on when a new world beckoned:

> Why remain here [in Greece] to struggle for a piece of bread without any security for the future, without honor and independence? Why not open your eyes and see the good that awaits you; harden your heart and seek your fortune abroad, where so many of your countrymen already have made theirs?

> Why linger? To protect your parents? Today or tomorrow, whether their children are here or abroad, they will close their eyes forever. It will be better for you to leave home and send a little money to provide for them in their advancing years. Or are you waiting to cultivate the barren lands with the ploughshare and dig in the fields? Have you seen how much progress you have made thus far? [10]

If such pleas were not enough to persuade Greeks to come to America, more personal testimonials proved effective. After a while, many Greeks knew someone, whether a friend, relative, or acquaintance from their village, who had gone to America. Letters home were read eagerly by villagers thirsting to hear of the wonders, comfort, and riches that the immigrants' new lives had brought them. One man wrote to his former boss that in America

> the people work much and regularly, and rest only on Sunday. . . . This day that I am writing you is Sunday; I took my bath, had my milk, and I will pass the day satisfactorily. Where did I know life with such order? . . . If you wish afentiko [master], you can do well to come, and I will send you the cost of the ticket.[11]

Some immigrants even enclosed photographs of themselves to show their new prosperity. Residents of the small villages read newspaper clippings containing reports of weddings, baptisms, or other important news of those who had gone to America. Money sent home by Greeks in America also helped encourage prospective immigrants. During the 1890s, the sum of a hundred American dollars (approximately two thousand dollars today) was a small fortune to Greeks living in poor villages and farms.

Other immigrants were drawn to America by something more than money. For many, the possibility of acquiring an education was enough to make them brave the unknown and journey to the United States. After the Second World War several thousand Greek students who wished to pursue advanced degrees began to arrive in the United States. Many of these students later applied for permanent residency or became American citizens. As a result, the Greek American community experienced the growth of a professional class, composed of doctors, lawyers, scientists, teachers, and the like.

A family of Greek peasants sits amid the ruins of their home, destroyed by Nazi invaders.

Legislation Helps

In the years following the Second World War, the U.S. government took steps to allow more immigrants, particularly refugees, or people whose homelands had been devastated in the war, to come to America. Both pieces of legislation—the Displaced Persons Act of 1948 and the Refugee Relief Act passed in 1953—made it easier for Greeks, many of whom had lost their homes and livelihoods because of the civil war, to enter the country. By the 1950s, a second wave of Greek immigrants was taking advantage of this opportunity and, as a result, the number of Greeks in the United States rose dramatically. Greek American associations, working with other national and ethnic groups, continued to lobby Congress to relax immigration restrictions and allow even more Greeks to enter the country. Congress did pass additional laws that permitted Greeks who already had family in America to settle in the United States. During the late 1960s the rise to power of an oppressive regime in Greece spawned another generation of Greek immigrants. Immigration reform made entering the United States even easier.

Most of the Greek immigrants who have come to the United States since the Second World War have come to stay. They include a greater number of women and educated professionals. Government estimates suggest that more than a million Greeks left their native land between 1950 and 1975, with approximately two hundred thousand leaving their villages, towns, and farms to come to the United States.

Once they had made the difficult decision to begin life anew in the United States, many began to ask themselves whether they could afford to make the journey across the sea.

CHAPTER THREE

Coming to America

For the majority of Greeks, coming to America was not easy. The journey itself was filled with uncertainty and hardship, and, of course, the immigrants left behind loved ones and familiar sights. Still, these difficulties did not stop the shepherds, merchants, artisans, fishermen, workers, and farmers who came by the hundreds of thousands to the New World.

The first wave of Greek immigration drew people from throughout Greece, including the Greek islands as well as the mainland peninsula. Many immigrants also hailed from Turkish-occupied territory. A small percentage of Greek immigrants came to America from Central Europe and North Africa, where established Greek communities had existed for years. The majority came from rural areas. Most had little or no schooling, and practically none spoke English. But no matter what their background was, all were ready to leave their homeland in the hope of finding success and wealth in the United States.

The High Cost of Travel

In addition to the emotional costs, the journey to America cost a great deal of money, and some Greeks who owned land or livestock sold off their holdings to buy passage to the United States. In addition, U.S.

Immigrants huddle together on deck in the steerage class of a ship bound for the United States. Travel to America was extremely expensive.

immigration law required that all adults coming to America have the equivalent of at least twenty-five dollars when they entered the country, which added significantly to the traveling expenses, for many Greeks were very poor.

In some cases, relatives already settled in America sent money for other family members to make the journey. For example, tickets to America for Bessie Spylios and her brother were paid out of wages sent by the children's father and older sister, who had left a year earlier. Michael Pappas, who became a successful American businessman,

had been given money by his grandmother. There was also one other option available to raise money for the trip to America: borrowing. Borrowing, in fact, became the most popular means of raising money for the journey to America, despite the high interest rates that moneylenders charged.

The Padrone

Those who had no money or relatives to help them relied on labor agents known as padrones, or "bosses," who recruited Greek immigrants to work in America. These agents, often Greeks themselves, visited towns and villages advertising for people who wanted to go to America. The padrones paid for people's passage in exchange for a promise to work for a certain employer in the United States. To further their effort, the padrones established ties with prominent local families in Greece. They were godfathers at christenings or best men at weddings. Everywhere they went, the padrones described the wonderful opportunities and great wealth available in the United States. They then indicated a willingness to provide transportation and work for anyone going to America to make a fortune. Many Greeks, but especially young, unmarried men, leapt at the opportunity the padrones offered.

Although it was difficult to part with their children, many parents felt relief at sending a son to work in the United States, for it meant one fewer mouth to feed at home. They also hoped that the boy would have a chance for a better life. As a result, few passed on a padrone's offer, and many young men found themselves on their way to America.

The contract Greek immigrants signed with a padrone was usually simple. Because few families could afford to pay passage from Greece, padrones advanced the money with the understanding that upon arrival in the United States, the young man would work for him or for another designated employer for a year. Often the padrone placed a mortgage on the family home against the son's earnings. If the young man broke the contract, not only did he forfeit his wages, but the family lost its home as well. Besides a job, the padrone promised to provide food and lodging. Jobs ordinarily ranged from a factory or a meat packinghouse to providing labor in a mine or on the railroad. Often, however, the padrones were unscrupulous and dishonest. They did not give immigrants the promised necessities and seized their wages as additional collateral to cover the costs of passage.

Leaving Home

Once a person had secured the means to leave, it was necessary to make arrangements on a steamship. To make travel as

The First to Leave

The Spartans were the first big group of Greeks to leave, emigrating to the United States in the early 1870s, with the wave peaking between 1890 and 1910. It was estimated that nearly three-fourths of the entire male population of Sparta between the ages of eighteen and thirty-five left to go to America. In many Spartan villages, this mass exodus was viewed with distress and fear, and many believed that their province had been cursed. Even though the typical immigrant was a married man who expected to return to his family, there were also a large number of single men, whose future was more uncertain. One local newspaper, alarmed at the growing numbers of male emigrants, pleaded with the Greek government to better conditions before too many men had left, putting the country in worse shape than before.

efficient and as profitable as possible, steamship companies involved themselves from the beginning to the end of an immigrant's journey. This participation was also a response to increasingly restrictive immigration laws passed in the United States, which made steamship lines assume the responsibility for the immigrants before and during their journey. Moreover, the shipping companies had to pay the costs of deporting any immigrants who did not meet the physical or mental requirements for entry into the country. These procedures could prove costly. Moreover, in 1903, companies were fined ten dollars for each immigrant U.S. officials turned away. Two years later, in 1905, the fine was raised to one hundred dollars. To avoid paying the fines, the steamship lines learned to take better care of their passengers to make sure they were healthy upon arrival.

A physician hired by a shipping line examined prospective immigrants. Those the doctor pronounced healthy and fit for travel were then required to make a deposit toward the purchase of a ticket, which for passage in steerage averaged between $30 and $36, the equivalent of $629 to $754 in today's currency. Company agents then issued a certificate stating that a reservation had been made in the person's name.

As the immigrants prepared to leave home, there was a flurry of activity. First there was the calendar to consider, as many Greek immigrants tried not to leave during the forty days of fasting done before Easter and Christmas. Mothers anxiously prepared their sons for the trip. Harry Kambouris remembers the emotional goodbye from his mother: "[She] kissed me, em-braced me, and gave me a handkerchief to remember her by and inside was a five drachma coin and a sprig of basil."[12] Other mothers sewed amulets, good luck charms, packets that might include a religious relic, a bit of garlic or a blue bead to ward off evil, a dried basil leaf or a piece of thyme for remembrance, and finally a small amount of Greek earth, to be sprinkled upon the family member if he or she should die while in America.

As the day of departure neared, entire villages became excited. The night before leaving, travelers spent time with family and friends. The men would drink ouzo, a strong Greek liquor, and sing songs and propose toasts to the immigrants. On the morning of departure, the entire village might turn out to say goodbye to those on their way to America. Many immigrant men wore new cheap suits; others were dressed in worn hand-me-downs. Some men wore the more traditional Greek costume of the black, baggy *vrakes,* a type of pants, and wore fringed kerchiefs on their heads. Still others wore the white pleated kilt favored by Greeks living on the mainland. What possessions they could carry were wrapped in blankets or tucked inside cheap cardboard suitcases. Before leaving the village, the immigrants stopped at the church, where they were blessed by the priest. Then, accompanied by their friends, they began their journey to *ksenita,* "the foreign place."

First Stop

After saying their goodbyes, the immigrants met steamship company officials,

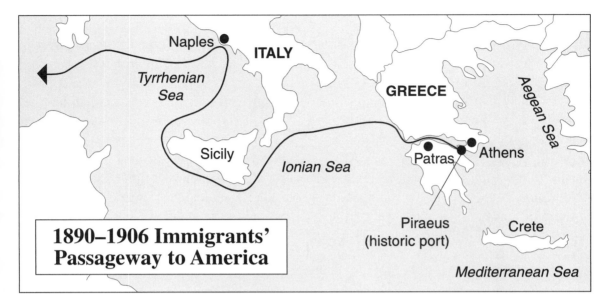

1890–1906 Immigrants' Passageway to America

who transported the travelers to the nearest railroad station, where chartered trains waited to take them to a port. Many steamship lines had regional ticket agencies and subagencies scattered throughout Greece. Here, local agents helped immigrants plan their journey from the village or city to the port at which the company's ships were docked.

For many Greek immigrants, the first stop on the long journey to America was to Piraeus, located approximately 6.2 miles southwest of Athens and one of the few major shipping and financial centers in Greece.

Once the trains arrived at their destination, whether Piraeus or another major port such as Kalamata or Patras, the immigrants waited until the ship on which they were to travel was ready to sail. This could mean a stay of a few days or a few weeks, depending on the circumstances. To accommodate the large numbers of persons waiting to sail, major shipping companies built small "villages" near the docks. Here immigrants could bathe, eat, and rest before boarding the ship. The accommodations were usually free or so cheap that most travelers could afford them. This arrangement also protected naive country people from losing their way, falling prey to unscrupulous ticket agents or thieves and other criminals who might rob, cheat, or even kill the unsuspecting travelers. For those who could afford it, cheap hotels and boardinghouses near the docks offered relatively inexpensive rooms and meals.

In addition to providing a place to stay while waiting to sail, the ship companies gave immigrants a second medical examination and an antiseptic bath intended to remove germs. Men and boys received short haircuts and had their scalps shampooed with a mixture of soft soap, creolin, carbolic acid, and petroleum to remove head lice and any other parasites or disease-causing microbes. Women, too, had their hair carefully shampooed and treated, though they escaped the barbers' shears. All who passed the second examination were allowed to complete the purchase of their ticket.

Shipping Out!

On the day of departure, all immigrants again underwent a medical examination at the shipping company offices. As they passed this final procedure, a company representative stamped their wrists with one of seven stamps, the meaning of which was kept secret until the ship set sail. At departure, the captain received a sealed envelope that contained a document notifying him of the stamp used for that journey. No one was permitted to board the ship whose wrist stamp and ticket did not match the identification mark the company had selected. This arrangement prevented passengers from switching identities, which was commonly attempted. The ink used for the stamps was impossible to wash off, which also discouraged people from trying to change places.

Before leaving, all immigrants signed statements acknowledging that they had no criminal record and documenting the amount of cash they carried. These questions were similar to those they would have to answer upon arriving in the United States. While the immigrants boarded the ship, their baggage, which had been stored in a company warehouse, was now inspected, stamped, and thoroughly disinfected before being placed aboard. Finally the days and weeks of waiting were over. The immigrants were on their way.

The Journey Across

By the time the first large wave of Greek immigrants arrived in America, the steamship companies were legally obliged to provide for each adult passenger 100 cubic feet of space, or roughly an area 5 feet wide, 5 feet long, and 4 feet high, on the upper steerage deck of the ship, 120 cubic feet was required on the lower steerage deck, an area approximately 5 feet wide, 5 feet long, and 5 feet high. A ship carrying more than fifty passengers had to be equipped with an infirmary and a doctor. Three meals a day were to be provided for each passenger, to be served at a table, and adequate hygiene and sanitation facilities were mandated.

The conditions on board many steamships, however, often did not come close to meeting the legal requirements. The majority of immigrants traveled in "steerage," so called because the passengers were housed on the bottom level of the ship, along with the steering mechanism. These quarters ran the entire length and width of the ship. An American immigration official who described them in 1911 noted that conditions did not meet legal standards. The immigrants' berths, or sleeping quarters, were

> dismal, damp, dirty, and [a] most unwholesome place. The air was heavy, foul, and deadening to the spirit and the mind. Those confined to these beds by reason of sickness soon lost all energy, spirit and ambition. . . . Such surroundings could not produce the frame of mind with which it is desirable that newcomers approach our land and receive their first impressions of it. [13]

Similarly, an American journalist writing in 1906 noted that "if human beings are to be subjected to treatment and conditions proper for cattle, then they should be taken at freight or live stock rates; or, on the other hand, if they are to be called passengers and charged a substantial passenger rate, then they should have the consideration of such." [14]

It was from the passengers traveling in steerage that the ship companies expected to make the greatest profit, since they provided minimal accommodations at the lowest possible costs and charged high fares. The companies outfitted the steerage decks with only the barest essentials. For very little money, they furnished iron frame bunks,

Immigrants to America like these endured severe overcrowding and unsanitary conditions in steerage class.

inexpensive blankets, which were often the kind used for horses, straw mattresses, and a variety of cheap tin cups, plates, bowls, and utensils. With the going rate of passage to America averaging less than $40 (or $838 in today's currency) and the company often crowding as many as a thousand passengers into steerage for one voyage, the profits to be made were enormous.

Some lines even converted old cattle boats into passenger vessels. The ships were outdated and, as Sam Fortosis, who came to the United States in 1914, recalled, notoriously slow and hard to handle. "The boats . . . they used to call them cattle boats. It took thirty days to cross the Atlantic. Plus a couple of days from Greece to Italy. . . . Because of the rough sea, the boat couldn't go ahead. In fact, it was four or five days

that we were going backward instead of forward." [15]

Life on Shipboard

Life on board ship during the journey across the Atlantic soon developed its own rhythm. Passengers settled into steerage and tried to get used to the various pipes and valves and the constant droning whir of the ship's engines. The bunks were uncomfortable, the straw mattresses misshapen and scratchy. The travelers slept with only a thin blanket to keep them warm; there were no pillows or sheets. Many companies, however, provided each steerage passenger with a life preserver, which immigrants sometimes placed under their heads at night.

"The Awfulness of Steerage Conditions"

In 1911 the U.S. Immigration Commission sent undercover agents to report on steerage conditions on a number of major steamship lines. The following is the conclusion of one agent's report on all the steerage berths, published as "Steerage Conditions," by the U.S. Immigration Commission later that year. This excerpt is found in Mary Shapiro's book Gateway to Liberty.

To sum up, let me make some general statements that give an idea of the awfulness of steerage conditions on the steamer. . . . During these twelve days in the steerage I lived in a disorder and in surroundings that offended every

sense. Only the fresh breeze from the sea overcame the sickening odors. The vile language of the men, the screams of women defending themselves, the crying of the children, wretched because of their surroundings, and practically every sound that reached the ear irritated beyond endurance. There was no sight before which the eye did not prefer to close. Everything was dirty, sticky, and disagreeable to the touch. Every impression was offensive. . . . For fifteen hours each day I witnessed all around me [the] . . . forced mingling of men and women who were total strangers and often did not understand one word of the same language.

Steerage was notoriously crowded. It was common for more persons to be crammed into steerage than was permitted by law. Some ship companies took account of special circumstances, providing women and small children with their own section, while confining men to another. Other ships had "marriage quarters," where families and small children could travel together. Young, single women traveling alone often stayed together in one part of the steerage quarters and tried to look after each other's welfare.

The floors in steerage were wood, which the crew swept every morning and then sprinkled lightly with sand to absorb moisture. The floors were never washed at sea and so became quite filthy. As one U.S. immigration agent noted, "There are no accommodations to encourage the steerage passenger to be clean and orderly. There was . . . no receptacle for refuse . . . no cans for use in case of seasickness."[16]

Each passenger was responsible for the dishes, bowls, and utensils provided to him or her by the ship company. If such items were lost or stolen, persons either shared with someone else or ate with their hands. Steerage passengers also had to wash their own dishes and utensils. This was easier said than done. In steerage, there was only one faucet that provided warm water for hundreds of people. When the faucet was unavailable, passengers washed their dishes in cold salt water from the sea. Because the dishes and utensils were of poor quality, however, the salt water soon damaged them so that they became unfit for use.

Meal times were rarely pleasant. People crowded into a large dining area filled with tables. The kitchen crew carried the food in pails or galvanized tin cans and ladled it into large serving bowls that they then placed on the tables. One immigrant remembered that when soup was served the ship's floor was all wet because so much had spilled. Since persons served themselves, those who were old or not feeling well might not get any food unless someone helped them. Immigrants who found ship food too strange and different from the kinds of food they had grown up with might instead refuse to eat it, relying for the entire trip on bread or cheese brought from home.

Adding to the unpleasantness of the journey for those traveling in steerage was the odor of so many sweaty bodies and the ever-present products of seasickness, which especially in the heat made breathing and sometimes eating quite difficult. What water was available was often fetid or at least tasted bad and gave some people stomachaches. Bad weather sometimes compounded these difficulties. In addition to the dangers of being caught in an Atlantic storm, foul weather made it impossible to leave steerage and to walk on deck to get fresh air. While some people passed the time talking, smoking, or playing cards, others sat quietly. One writer aboard a ship described a group of Greek immigrants who were traveling to America:

Many of them left their village for the first time and for the first time had seen the ocean which terrified them even when it was calm. They were melancholy and sat in small groups and spoke slowly. Every one of them

This nineteenth-century drawing shows immigrants passing the time on their way to America. Fine weather allowed immigrants to enjoy the open air on deck.

must have been thinking of the village he left behind, his wife, his children, his parents. [17]

When the weather was good, however, everyone ventured to the upper steerage decks. Those who had brought musical instruments with them gave impromptu concerts. Others joined in native songs and dances. Children ran and played, while their parents and other adults talked or just walked about enjoying the sea air and the sunshine. One young immigrant woman re-membered seeing dolphins swimming beside the ship one day as she ventured out on deck. Everyone made the most of the fresh air, for passengers never knew when bad weather would set in and send them below again.

America!

Depending on the route, the weather, and the speed of the ship, the journey to America could last anywhere from six days to two weeks. No matter how long it took, the first glimpse of the United States was among the most memorable moments in the life of a Greek immigrant. Seeing the Statue of Liberty signaled to many that their long voyage was nearly at an end and their new life in America was about to begin. They had asked for an opportunity to show that they, too, could succeed, as had others before them. But before immigrants could embark on their American adventure, there was a final and, for some, a frightening obstacle: passing through the gates of Ellis Island to learn whether officials would allow them to enter the United States.

CHAPTER FOUR

Ellis Island

With the awesome sights and sounds of the New York harbor in the background, many immigrants nervously awaited their arrival at the Ellis Island immigration station. Irene Meladaki Zambelli, who came to the United States in 1914, recalls the scene on shipboard when she first arrived:

> We finally arrived in New York. . . . There was no more seasickness and we got ready to get off the ship. We were all dressed up. . . . I had a very pretty suit and an embroidered blouse under it and a little hat to match the suit. . . . My shoes were also custom made with high top buttons, the bottoms patent leather and the tops suede. . . . The rest of the women on the ship were mountain women with handkerchiefs on their heads. Everyone looked bad [from having been] seasick.[18]

For many immigrants, seasickness had been replaced with worry. It was here at Ellis Island that the final decision would be made: Would they or would they not be allowed to stay in the country? But besides the fear, there was also excitement and curiosity about this new land they had traveled so far to reach.

Ellis Island Welcomes Greek Immigrants

When the Dutch explorer Henry Hudson made the first recorded sighting of what became Ellis Island in 1609, it was little more than three acres across. Over time its size increased, thanks to landfill projects, to its present area: 27.5 acres. For Greek immigrants arriving in the United States in the mid-1890s, the buildings located on Ellis Island were still new, having opened their doors on January 1, 1892.

The centerpiece of the new immigration station was an impressive three-story structure described in a popular magazine of the time as "a latter-day watering palace hotel, presenting to the view a great many-windowed expanse of buff-painted wooden walls, of blue slate roofing, and of light and picturesque towers."[19] The complex also included a hospital, a powerhouse, a surgeon's quarters, a bathhouse, and a detention center. In fact, between 1901 and 1910, nearly 7 million immigrants passed through Ellis Island, representing roughly today's population of the five boroughs of New York City. For the immigrants who came through its doors, Ellis Island was the symbolic gateway to America.

Immigrant children stage a parade celebrating America at Ellis Island.

First Steps in America

Once the ship had docked in New York harbor, immigration officers from Ellis Island, including landing inspectors and a medical officer, came aboard. They first examined the cabin-class passengers for identification and signs of illness. These examinations were often cursory because cabin-class passengers generally had more money and were considered to be a better kind of people than those who traveled steerage. Most cabin-class travelers passed through quickly; only a few were detained and sent to Ellis Island. This fact had not gone unnoticed by the immigrants; those who thought they or a family member might not pass the more stringent examinations conducted at Ellis Island bought a second-class cabin ticket. All others, the steerage passengers, had to wait below deck until they were told to leave the ship. If the officials at Ellis Island were particularly busy, those still on board might have to wait for days to receive permission to disembark.

Upon leaving the ship, the immigrants were packed onto small ferryboats that took

Immigrants celebrate when they catch their first glimpse of the Statue of Liberty as their ship sails into New York harbor.

them to Ellis Island, where they waited again until officials gave them permission to enter the main building for physical examinations and final processing. Based on the ship's manifest, or passenger list, the immigrants were placed in groups of thirty. Each group was directed to a baggage room, where the people were instructed to leave their belongings. Immigrants then found themselves in a large, dark, tiled entrance corridor, where they were directed toward a flight of stairs that led to the second floor Registry Hall. Watching the immigrants from the top of the stairs were officials from the U.S. Public Health Service. They performed the "six-second medical examination," scanning the crowd for individuals who were having trouble climbing the stairs, which could reveal a number of symptoms that warranted closer examination.

At the top of the stairs, the immigrants entered the Registry Hall, certainly one of the largest rooms most had ever seen. Measuring 200 feet long by 100 feet wide, with a 56-foot vaulted ceiling, the Registry Hall was divided into a maze of passageways in which immigrants underwent a series of examinations to assess their mental and physical health. Failure to meet certain standards could result in deportation. On any given day, thousands of hopeful and nervous persons from around the world passed through the Registry Hall. Outside were rows of wooden benches where immigrants spent hours awaiting their turn to enter. To one side of the Registry Hall were dormitories for those who needed medical attention, were quarantined, or were being detained until they could be sent back home. The dormitories were overcrowded, dirty, and noisy.

Spotting Suspicious Cases

On any given day, the doctors at Ellis Island had to make a decision in a matter of minutes about each of the thousands of immigrants who passed through. One local representative of an immigrant aid society recalled in an interview quoted in David M. Brownstone, Irene M. Franck, and Douglass Brownstone's book, Island of Hope, Island of Tears, *that the doctors relied on a number of "tricks" that helped them quickly diagnose the many immigrants who came before them.*

The doctor would have them put their hands down on the desk and if they showed pink, he passed them as not suffering from a heart condition. But when the nails were very blue we put them aside as a heart case. When a man came in with a very thin, stringy beard they thought there was some lack of physical development. . . . When someone walked and hesitated and constantly looked down on the ground to see where he was, they knew that he had trouble with his eyes. . . . When a woman was pregnant, for some reason she always had disheveled hair . . . they knew there was something wrong with those women.

A Special Code

The medical examination in the Registry Hall was conducted by a doctor with the U.S. Public Health Service. The exam usually lasted

A health official examines immigrant children upon their arrival to Ellis Island. Doctors were careful to search for signs of disease.

two to three minutes. As each person stepped before the doctor, an interpreter standing nearby asked questions about age, general health, origins, and destination, while the doctor examined the individual's face, neck, hands, and hair, giving careful attention, as well, to pos-

ture, walk, and eyes. According to one observer, although the examination was quick, it was comprehensive:

> We used to like to have passengers while under inspection make two right

angle turns. The scheme served to bring the light on both sides of a passenger's face. The turns also helped to bring out imperfections in muscular coordination and this also together with the facial expression, posture and perhaps evidence of indifference to personal appearance, served to make the detection of abnormal mental conditions easier. [20]

During their examinations, doctors were especially careful to search for signs of certain diseases, in particular, favus, a fungal disease of the scalp, and trachoma, an inflammation of the eyes that, if left untreated, could cause blindness. Both diseases were common among immigrants from southern Europe, were highly contagious, and were difficult to cure. They were also virtually unknown in the United States, which explains the determination of health officials to prevent their spread. The test for trachoma was painful. Doctors pulled each eyelid up and over a buttonhook to inspect it. After a person's eyes had been examined and disinfected to prevent the outbreak of disease, he or she moved on to the next station.

The doctors at Ellis Island used a coded letter system as a shorthand to indicate any medical problems that required further attention. Immigrants identified as having visible health problems had their clothing marked with chalk. An "H" meant heart trouble. "Ct" signified trachoma. An "F" signaled a foot problem. An "X" meant that the person was mentally defective, while "Pg" symbolized pregnancy, and an "S" denoted senility.

"Chalked"

Everyone who had been marked with chalk was taken out of line and moved to another area that consisted of a series of wire compartments, or "cages." Here doctors conducted a more thorough medical examination to determine the state of the immigrant's health and to identify any condition that might warrant deportation. If it was determined that there were no serious problems, the person was allowed to return to the main line for processing. However, if doctors believed that a serious ailment or mental problem was present, they sent the person to the hospital for further study, treatment, or, in the most extreme cases, deportation. Estimates indicate that between 15 and 20 percent of each group of immigrants that came through Ellis Island had a medical problem, often a serious one.

As much as the eye test, immigrants dreaded being "chalked." Family members, already anxious, became even more so if a child or older relative was pulled out of the line. Often family members were separated, not knowing whether they all would be together again in America.

The Legal Examination

Those who were certified as healthy were led to another area, where an immigration official awaited them. He questioned the immigrants about the relationships of the men and women in the family. This procedure was designed to identify women who might be of "questionable" moral character, such as prostitutes. If questions were answered satisfactorily, the official directed the group to another waiting area near a series of desks.

When a registry clerk was ready, a group was called forward, and the people were told to form a straight line. Then each person waited his or her turn to appear before the clerk and answer more questions. Many of the questions were similar to those that representatives of the steamship company had asked back in Greece. Essentially, immigration officials wanted to know whether the newcomers had sufficient means to support themselves in the United States. Did they have family with whom they could reside? Did they have a job? Did they know how to find one? The examiner also asked questions intended to identify individuals who might threaten the security of the country or pose a danger to the public.

As with the medical examinations, the clerks took about two minutes to decide whether a person was fit to stay in the United States. Jacob Riis, a Scandinavian immigrant and newspaper reporter, reflected as he watched the busy clerks in 1903 that

> there seems to be no language or dialect under the sun that does not lie handy to the tongue of these men at the desk. There were twelve of them. One would never dream there were twelve such linguists in the country till he hears them and sees them; for half their talk is done with their hands and shoulders and with the official steel pen that transfixes an object of suspicion like a merciless spear.[21]

Besides asking personal questions, clerks asked immigrants to do simple arithmetic. Immigrants then had to show proof that they had some money. Adult immigrants had to have the equivalent of 25 American dollars to be allowed to stay. Irene Meladaki Zambelli who came to the United States from Greece in 1914 at the age of twenty-four described the questions that she and her cousin had to answer:

> We came to the next gate and they asked us how much was two and two and four and four. We answered and went to the next gate. They asked us how much money we had. We had between us $30 in gold money. We proudly showed off the money and they hung a plaque with a number around our neck [to identify the train route they were to board] and told us to keep going. . . . One man when they asked how much is two and two, he did not know and my cousin kept nudging him and repeating "Four, four, four." Finally the man said "Four," and they let him go. Then I heard screams and a woman crying, saying "Yes, she is my daughter! She is my daughter!". . . she had given her age to be younger than her daughter's. They were both crying for fear they would be sent back. I said to the daughter, "Tell your mother to try to remember her age because she could not be your mother if she is younger than you."[22]

The "Stairs of Separation"

Finally, those who had answered all questions to the satisfaction of the officials were allowed to leave, their "landing cards" (a document that certified they were in Amer-

Immigrants sit on numbered benches at Ellis Island, waiting to be processed for entry into the United States.

ica legally) in hand. These immigrants were then escorted to an area on the other side of the registry desk, also known as the "stairs of separation." Here families and friends could be separated within minutes as those who were allowed to stay in the country went on their way, while family members or friends who had not passed the oral examinations were left behind to be detained or even deported. One visitor noted that the manner in which families were divided "seems heartless, but it is the only practical system, for if allowance was made for goodbyes the examination and distribution process would be blocked then and there by a dreadful crush. Special officers would be necessary to tear relatives forcibly from each other's arms."[23] From start to finish the entire process of going through Ellis Island could take two to three hours or as long as an entire day.

There were three ways for immigrants to go when they at last had passed through the most difficult obstacles. Those bound for New York City followed a stairway that led to a lower level and then to an area where family and friends might be waiting. For the majority of immigrants, however, the next destination was a large hall where they could change their money into U.S. currency and purchase train tickets to travel to points west. Those bound for the New England states entered a room to the left to make travel arrangements.

There was also a fourth area, where no immigrants wished to go: This room brought them before another immigration official, who sat in front of a barred gate that guarded the entrance to the detention room. The would-be immigrants sent here were those who had not made it past the doctors and registry clerks. Those who were sick or lacked money were deported. So were those thought to be physically or mentally incapable of earning a living and those tagged as potential political or public menaces. Foreign governments also on occasion requested that a runaway spouse or child, or a criminal, be detained and then deported. Women traveling alone were often detained until immigration officials could determine whether they had family or friends in the United States who could look after their welfare. One young Greek woman, Bessie Spylios, stayed at Ellis Island for almost

Women Alone

The preferred way for women to come to America was in the company of a male relative or spouse. In fact, the Greek government after 1920 specifically forbade women and girls under sixteen from traveling unless they were accompanied by a parent or male guardian. But not all women were able to travel this way. The experience could be a difficult one, as writer Helen Zeese Papanikolas describes in this excerpt from the book Greek Americans *by Charles C. Moskos.*

Such women suffered not only from the fear of coming alone to a country whose language they did not know, but from violating the rigid code of their people. In the Mediterranean countries where a poor man's only possessions were his self-respect and his daughter's virginity, women were chaperoned with paranoid obsession. Women traveling alone to America were tragically burdened with the anxiety that they would be suspected forever of having questionable morals.

two days until her father could come and get her and her brother:

> I wasn't concerned. I was young and I didn't care. I knew he was going to come. And a special woman talked to us in Greek and we felt more secure. We knew we were in the right place and that our father was going to come. . . . What [a] place that was! Beautiful. . . . Balconies on top, you know, all the way around and people who had to wait a long time could go upstairs and watch the people downstairs. And they had cots where I slept. . . . [It was] a nice clean place. I can't forget how clean that place was.[24]

For the immigrants who had successfully passed through Ellis Island, approximately 98 percent of those who had arrived there, it was now time to get on with the business of being in America. For some, including many Greeks, this meant shedding their foreign-looking clothing. If they were going to live in America, the newcomers intended to look like Americans and dress like Americans. Edward Corsi, a former commissioner at Ellis Island, described the sight:

> Many people have told me that half an hour after the boat came in, the dressing rooms in the adjacent ferry houses, the bushes at the lower end of Battery Park [at the southern tip of Manhattan] and even the gutters along the sidewalks presented the appearance of a junk shop. Queer headgear of women lay about, the familiar black-visored caps of the men and boys, waists [blouses] and skirts or coats and trousers [that] would not go far in Manhattan without causing comment and ridicule.[25]

For many of these immigrants, the transformation into Americans had begun before they left home, thanks to relatives and friends who had brought American clothing for the new arrivals to wear. For others, clothing had to wait. The task now at hand was to find a job and a home, so that they could properly begin their new life.

CHAPTER FIVE

Earning a Living

With Ellis Island behind them, Greek immigrants headed for various destinations in all parts of the country, including the western United States and the Alaska territory, determined to establish themselves in America. For those who had neither family nor friends to guide them, the first order of business was to find a job as quickly as possible, preferably one that did not require them to master English. In time, though, Greeks began forming their own communities.

For Greek immigrants who came to the United States before 1920, jobs were plentiful. Few wanted to farm or even acquire land of their own, since they associated farming with the hard times they had suffered in Greece. Alternately, they sought to live in towns and cities where other Greeks resided. The lure of a steady paycheck also drew the majority of Greek immigrants to urban centers large and small.

Making Their Way

Despite the inability of many to speak English, Greek immigrants brought with them a determination to succeed and a willingness to work hard. But they also realized that to succeed in America meant starting at the bottom, working at menial jobs for little pay. And despite their attraction to cities, many found the quick tempo of urban life unsettling and disorienting. Yet, many soon realized that if they were to make something of themselves, they needed to get used to how things were done in America.

The Greek immigrants who spoke little or no English had difficulty with daily life. Asking directions or finding work was sometimes very complicated. While some Greeks attended English classes, others taught each other the words they had learned while at work. Some, particularly

A Greek woman struggles to read an English text in a classroom. Learning English was a challenge for many Greek immigrants.

the older women who rarely left home, never bothered to learn English. But many who took jobs soon learned that an inability to speak English meant that they had no chance to get a promotion.

The first paying jobs in the United States for many Greeks came in what were known as the "petty street trades." They worked for vendors who sold flowers, candy, or cigars. After they had been in America for a while, some Greeks who had accumulated small sums of money opened boardinghouses or small taverns that served the Greek immigrant community. Among Americans, Greek immigrants soon earned a reputation as skillful, successful merchants. As one Washington, D.C. reporter noted in 1904: "Not everyone knows that ninety-nine of every hundred of itinerant vendors is a Greek and that every Georgios or Demetrios among them, boy or man . . . is a small capitalist, and carries anywhere from fifty to several hundred dollars concealed about his person."[26]

Thousands of Greeks also made their living by working in the textile mills of Massachusetts. They impressed factory owners with their diligence and willingness to work under the rough and dangerous conditions of the early plants. Soon supervisors were asking the Greeks if they knew of others who needed jobs. As a result, more Greeks came to the mill towns. In general, the Greeks who worked in the mills tended to stay at those jobs rather than to establish themselves in business. For some, the mills were the easiest and quickest way to make money so they could return to Greece. Starting a business meant a commitment that for some Greeks was not desirable. For those whose primary goal was to make enough money to eventually return home and live in relative comfort, mill work represented the best alternative.

Greek immigrants also worked as bootblacks or shoe shiners, waiters, dishwashers, cooks, and clerks in restaurants and stores whose customers were mainly immigrants. Some learned a trade such as bricklaying or woodworking. Those lucky enough to have arrived with money opened restaurants, grocery stores, coffeehouses, taverns, salons, barbershops, shoe-shine parlors, print shops, and brokerage firms. The Greeks soon learned that they could compete with American and other immigrant businesses, and in time many abandoned street peddling and opened their own stores. They began by doing business in the Greek community, but eventually broadened their clientele to include non-Greeks as well. The fact that many Greeks came from peasant backgrounds makes their business success stories all the more remarkable.

Although their numbers were not significant, there were some Greek doctors and lawyers who offered their services to the Greek community. Doctors serving Greek patients did not have to speak English well. Lawyers, however, needed to speak and write English, and to understand American laws. Also, Greek-born lawyers had to pass a state bar examination before they could practice law in the United States. Those unable to master the language or pass the required exam were obliged to find another line of work.

The "Thalassocracy"

A small number of Greek immigrants earned a living fishing or diving for sponges. Greek fishing communities were scattered throughout the country; but some of the larger ones were found in Florida, where Greeks worked as sponge divers; in Rhode Island, where many fished for lobsters; and in California, where they caught lobsters and other kinds of seafood. Fishermen working along the Sacramento River in northern California also established the first Greek fishermen's association in the United States. Some Greeks joked about the rise of a "Thalassocracy," from the Greek words for "sea" and "class of powerful persons." The ancient Greeks had enjoyed command over large expanses of the seas, but the Greeks in California were content to begin on a much smaller scale.

Working for the Padrone

Despite their willingness to work hard for low pay, many Greek immigrants suffered exploitation at the hands of unscrupulous business owners. Perhaps the most notorious form of abuse was the padrone system. Many Greeks, but especially those who arrived during the first wave of immigration, relied on the padrone to find them jobs, housing, and virtually everything else they needed to survive. Padrones wielded considerable power in the Greek immigrant community, and few thought of challenging them or questioning their judgment. In almost every city with a population of more than ten thousand, a padrone system had been established. For the Greeks, the padrones confined themselves to certain businesses including shoe-shine parlors and flower, fruit, and vegetable vending operations; in the western United States they controlled railroad construction crews.

For all the help he might extend to newly arrived immigrants, the padrone made sure he was compensated for his efforts, exacting a fee that was often exorbitant. The helpless immigrants had no choice but to pay. By placing immigrants in low-wage jobs, the padrone limited their ability to pay back the debt, guaranteeing that people would owe him for a long time to come. Sometimes the padrone left his workers only enough money to pay their room and board; anything beyond what they needed to meet necessary expenses went into his pocket. In essence, the padrone system was similar to indentured servitude, a common practice among the English colonists during the seventeenth and eighteenth centuries.

One of the most notorious Greek padrones was Leonidas G. Skliris. Skliris not only extorted large sums of money from Greek immigrants, he also supplied workers to companies for substandard pay. By undercutting going wage rates, Skliris made sure that the workers he represented would be the first hired. Then, too, Skliris brought in Greek immigrants to use as strikebreakers during labor disputes. These workers enabled company owners to keep factories operating after

This photograph from the early 1900s depicts the deplorable living conditions of immigrant workers. Despite their hard work, many Greek Americans lived in similar squalor.

the regular labor force had gone on strike. With the mills in full operation, owners had little incentive to negotiate with strikers.

For his troubles, Skliris took a cut from the paycheck of every worker for whom he found a job. Because of his power and notoriety, Skliris was nicknamed the "Czar of the Greeks." He was, to be sure, as tyrannical and ruthless as any czar, as those who opposed or resisted him quickly dis-

covered. Greek workers were afraid to speak out against him, for fear of losing their jobs. In 1911, fifty Greek workers wrote to the governor of Utah in an attempt to bring charges against Skliris. However, few volunteered to come forward and testify against their padrone; as one Greek laborer stated in the letter to the governor, "We are hungry and we don't want to die."[27]

Making a Living

By the mid-1890s, many recent Greek immigrants to the United States were at work in the shoe-shine trade, a business that African Americans and Italians had formerly dominated. Shoe shiners could be found everywhere in cities but were usually located near popular hotels, restaurants, and saloons. The business could consist of anything from a fancy shoe-shine parlor in a building to a simple outdoor booth or chair. Compared with other jobs, the requirements were simple: a strong back, a good pair of arms, and a willingness to work long, hard hours for little money. For many Greek immigrants, shining shoes was the perfect entry-level job, and soon they began to dominate the business.

Encouraged by their early successes, many parlor owners in large cities such as New York and Chicago began to organize their businesses into "chains." But to make money, the owners needed a steady supply of cheap labor, for which they turned to the padrones. In the beginning, finding prospective employees was easy, as the padrones steered the young men and boys they had recruited in Greece to work in the shoe-shine establishments. Under the padrone system, thousands of young Greek males, usually between fourteen and eighteen years of age, flocked to America. Upon arrival, they were instructed to report to a saloon or restaurant, where they would be apprenticed to shoe-shine parlors. Later, restaurant owners, peddlers, and fruit and flower vendors also acquired workers in this way. Hiring out apprentices through these "middle men"

helped the padrones to conceal their activities from the local authorities.

For many Greek boys, the new life in America was hard. They often worked fifteen hours a day, seven days a week shining shoes. After the business closed, they were responsible for cleaning the shop and laundering the shoe cloths.

A Hard Life

Like those at work in the shoe-shine business, the fruit and vegetable vendors started their days between five and six o'clock in the morning. Young boys went to apartment houses with samples of the produce they had to offer, while the padrone stayed behind to protect his wares from theft. Peddlers learned quickly that using young boys worked to their advantage, as women were more likely to let children into their homes than an adult vendor. When a sale was made, the boy returned to the padrone to pick up more fruit and vegetables and in this fashion worked his way through the neighborhood.

Boys working for padrones in the flower business were usually under sixteen years of age. While there were not as many of them as there were shoe-shine boys or fruit and vegetable vendors, they worked just as hard. Flower sales were usually conducted in city parks or on street corners. Boys employed by full-time florists, as opposed to boys hired by businesses that did a more limited business selling flowers, generally were better fed and more decently housed. Their wages could be anywhere from $50 to $100 a year, a princely sum by the standards of the time.

At Home

The Greek boys working for the fruit and vegetable vendors and the shoe-shine parlors had a hard life outside work, too. Almost all were poorly housed and fed. The boys sometimes slept in barns and stables or found lodging in filthy basements or overcrowded, unventilated spaces where they were crowded into tiny rooms, which often lacked heat and light. Commonly, three or four shared a single bed. Food and clothing were meager. Boys who worked for flower and fruit vendors were never really "off duty," for the unsold merchandise was stored where the boys lived, to be sold the following day.

The padrone maintained rigid control over his charges, forbidding them to learn English, censoring their mail, and even preventing them from talking to other Greeks in the neighborhood. One shoe-shine boy described the working conditions that he endured to an interviewer from the Humane Society of Cincinnati in 1911. According to the organization's report:

> His employer made him work from half-past six in the morning until eleven at night, took away his tips, half starved him, and refused to pay even his meager wages of thirty five cents per day until the end of the year to prevent his leaving. An investigation was made, and fifteen other boys were found to be living in the same conditions as the complainant.[28]

Making a Home

Living conditions varied from region to region, but in general accommodations were overcrowded and poor. In the mining towns and camps in the west, Greeks were crowded together in makeshift housing. Disease, particularly tuberculosis, was rampant, as was violence. Sometimes Greek workers were victims of hostility by native-born Americans. In other instances, old family or village feuds led to violent episodes among the Greek immigrants themselves. Greek immigrants living in the cities and factory towns were best characterized as frugal. Because approximately 95 percent of the Greeks who came to the United States were males who were saving money to send back home, many chose to rent a single apartment where as many as half a dozen men crowded together to share expenses.

Conditions were not much better for Greek families. Maria Tovas, who came to America in 1920, remembers the first time she saw the apartment her brother shared with five other young men. Each boy had a bed, but there was very little other furniture. A box underneath the bed held a boy's clothing. Doukenie Papandreos, who lived with her uncle when she first arrived, described her first house in America as consisting of only two rooms, with no shower or bathtub.

Since few apprentices could understand, much less read and write, English, the padrones exercised great control over their lives. Long hours made it impossible for them to go to school or to relax.

Despite the harsh conditions, many young apprentices were grateful to the padrone. They believed that if it were not for "the boss," they would starve to death, be sent back to Greece, or be killed. The wages that they did earn, usually between $10 and $20 a year, were more than they would have made back home. Few saw the system for what it really was: a vicious form of labor exploitation that kept them from earning decent wages and enjoying healthy working and living conditions.

The End of the Padrone System

Initially, many Greeks thought nothing was wrong with the padrone system. But by the early twentieth century, voices in the Greek community began to condemn the practice. "There are certain rich bosses who fill their teeth with gold," charged one editorial in the Greek-language newspaper *Saloniki,* "by the sweat and blood of young Greek boys."[29] Others called for laws to outlaw the padrone system.

By 1916, various organizations, such as the Employers Protective Association in Chicago, had formed to solve the problem. Owners and apprentices alike presented their grievances to the association, and, in many cases, reached agreements that resulted in better working conditions. But other forces were at work against the padrone system. The arrival of the auto-

mobile meant that fewer people walked and thus fewer dirtied their shoes, reducing the need for shoe shiners. Rising labor costs also caused a decline in the number of fruit, flower, and candy stores as smaller owners closed their shops. The growing power of American labor unions also influenced the decline of the padrone. More important, Greek workers adapted to American life and became less reliant on the padrone system. In so doing, they helped to put the padrones out of business.

Out West

For Greeks who did not want to work in the crowded cities, there was another alternative. According to figures released in 1907, approximately thirty to forty thousand Greeks journeyed west to find jobs. Two of the most advantageous places to seek employment were the many mines in the Rocky Mountain region, especially in Colorado and Utah, and on the railroad gangs found throughout the West. In some regions, such as California, Greeks made up the largest single ethnic group working on the railroads.

Unfortunately, many of these jobs were to be had through the padrone, putting the men in a position similar to that of their compatriots in the cities. In some cases, when an immigrant arrived at a rail camp, there was no job waiting for him. Or if there was, the worker would end up paying a number of "fees," such as an interpreter's fee, or a labor agent's fee, all of which went to the padrone.

In addition to having to pay bribes and other monies to the padrone, Greek workers faced bad treatment from the railroads. In 1915 a railroad gang of one hundred Greeks was transported from Chicago to Omaha, Nebraska, where the men were to begin work for the railroad. After working only two days, however, they were ordered to leave, with no explanation given. Finding themselves with no money in a place where they knew no one, the men went without food for an entire day and were forced to sleep in nearby fields. By the second day, the men were so desperate and angry that they began dismantling the railroad tracks they had laid only days earlier. The men were arrested, but a judge later ruled in their favor, not only freeing them but ordering the company to pay for their transportation back to Chicago.

Working the railroads was a harsh and hard life. One Greek immigrant, on his way out West in 1911, described the working situation of his fellow countrymen:

A Greek traveling by rail over these immense western states cannot but feel grief and sorrow . . . when he sees at nearly every mile of railway little groups of his own people with pick and shovel in their hands. All these have left their beloved fatherland, their families, their fellow countrymen, and their lands, and come here to build and repair railways in the hope of acquiring a few thousand [dollars] instead of which they acquire rheumatism, tuberculosis, venereal diseases, and those other ills, while others are deprived of feet, hands, eyes and some of their lives! This is unhappily the bitter truth. [30]

Working the railroads or in the mines was not for everyone. It was at best seasonal work as well as highly dangerous. Hundreds of immigrants were severely injured on the job, and several lost their lives. Under these circumstances, many ended up maimed or crippled. It was also known that many doctors were very quick to amputate limbs, and so injured Greeks often asked to be taken to one of their own folk healers. These healers would prescribe traditional Greek herbal remedies, which the men hoped would allow the wounds to heal and so eliminate the threat of amputation.

When it was too cold to continue working outdoors, many Greeks left the area, migrating to one of the nearest communities that had sprung up in cities like Chicago, Minneapolis, Omaha, and San Francisco. There they spent the winter months either waiting for the warmer weather to go back to work or seeking other employment. This practice allowed them an opportunity to take part in the local community life, catch up with the news, and eat some Greek cooking.

A Woman's Opportunity

Working opportunities for Greek women in America were few, for it was considered unseemly for Greek women, single or married, to work at all outside the home. Many considered this a sign that the male relatives or husband could not provide for the family. Many immigrant men, in fact, chose not to marry because they knew they could not raise a family unless the wife worked also. Nevertheless, many married Greek women helped their husbands establish

Immigrant laborers pose for a photo during construction of a railway. Many Greek immigrants found work on American railroads.

businesses such as restaurants and grocery stores, since family businesses were seen as acceptable. Some Greek women ran boardinghouses or took in laundry or sewing, which allowed them to stay at home. The greatest majority of women workers, though, were the single women, who flocked to the mills and textile factories in New England in search of work. But if an opportunity for marriage presented itself, the woman rarely returned to her job.

Some Greek women came over specifically to be married. These women became known as "picture brides" because they often carried with them a picture of their future bridegroom. Perhaps sent to America because there was no suitor or dowry for them at home, these Greek women, after weathering the trip to America, then traveled by train to destinations all over the country. Few wanted to end up as the only unmarried child in their family, for it was customary for unmarried women to act as unpaid servants to the rest of the family. Upon reaching their destination, the women would meet for the first time their future husbands. Sometimes, the bride would discover that the picture she had been sent did not match the face of the man she had agreed to marry. But in many cases, this made little difference; most women were just happy to be married. Sometimes these arrangements lacked the warmth and happiness of a traditional marriage, as one Greek woman later related:

When they arrived in America, grandfather took Mama to [her future mother-in-law's] home in New York City where they prepared for the wedding. Mama was not consulted about any of the arrangements. What should have been a beautiful time in her life was tempered by the unfriendly atmosphere around her. Soon after the wedding, she asked where she could find work to supplement my father's income. . . . She was given the address of a garment factory and the address of their apartment and put on a streetcar. [31]

Wanted: People to Work the Land

The majority of Greeks coming to the United States found little appeal in the idea of working again as farmers or herdsmen. But a small minority did continue working the land just as they had done in Greece. Many of these immigrants traveled to the western region of the United States, where they took up farming or raised sheep or cattle. They also found the area reminiscent of their home country with its many mountains, valleys, and rivers.

Some Greeks journeyed to the southern United States, where they too attempted to establish farms and small ranches. But they were less successful, encountering prejudice among the local residents and deciding that farming was just as unprofitable as it had been in Greece. Many of these immigrants then went to the cities to find work.

Still, booklets and pamphlets circulated in Greece advised future immigrants to think seriously of farming in the United States. These publications told Greeks that they had a better chance of making money in agriculture than in a factory or mill. Some local Greek immigrant newspapers, such as the *California*, which was published for the Greek community in San Francisco, also emphasized farming as a potential money-making occupation, stating "Cease having those rusty ideas that you came here to stay three or four years and return to your native country. You will never make enough money to return to your native country, unless you go into agriculture." The paper went on to advise that working and living in American cities was dangerous, expensive, and exhausting, and that the Greeks, who were a people of the land, would be content and happier working outside on their own farms. Despite these appeals, many Greeks decided to take their chances and go to the many American cities where they were certain better opportunities awaited them.

Many Greek immigrant women later spoke of the "homesickness that has no cure," in that they longed for their villages and families. Many women regretted particularly the loss of male relatives, who traditionally protected female members of the family from unwanted advances or abuse. In America, because the husband was often working long hours or was away at a job, women had to contend with being alone a great deal. For those who had to work, especially in the cities, making their way in a world that was both frightening and different only added to their uncertainty. Anastasia Triandafels Siouris, described her early life as the wife of a railroad worker:

I was the only Greek woman in the railroad town. I was so lonely that I baked cookies and sat on the porch waiting for the school children to come by. I had them eat the cookies and didn't understand what they were saying, but at least I heard the sound of human voices. [32]

Gradually, as Greek immigrants began to settle in the United States, they came together to form their own communities. Some cities, such as Chicago, had Greeks from every province. It was said that in Chicago, a Greek from any part of Greece was sure to find someone who spoke the same regional dialect. In time, though, many Greeks, while welcoming the company of others from their home country, wished for more. They had finally made it to America and had found a way to eke out a living; now it was time to establish themselves for good.

CHAPTER SIX

Living Greek, Becoming American

The transition to life in the United States was not always easy, as Greeks, like other immigrants, struggled to overcome language barriers and lack of immediately marketable skills. But unlike many other immigrant groups, the Greeks mastered the ability to absorb and adapt to other cultures, in part because of their long history of being conquered by other nations. Although approximately 80 percent of the Greek immigrants who arrived during the period from 1890 to 1920 came from rural areas, where many had worked as farmers or artisans, nearly all adapted to life in cities and towns, while learning new job skills. Another factor that helped many Greek immigrants to become more American was the similarity between Greek and American culture, both of which stress hard work, self-reliance, social commitment, and success.

In time, "Greektowns" began appearing, complete with Greek-owned businesses to serve the neighborhood. Like other immigrants, Greek Americans imported a variety of customs and institutions, such as restaurants, cafes, coffeehouses, taverns, and bakeries. These, along with certain customs and traditions, helped keep alive their Greek identity and recapture the close-knit sense of community that they had experienced in the "old country."

The Greek Press

Greek Americans enjoy a saying, "Either you give me a job or I'll bring out a newspaper."[33] Certainly, one of the most influential institutions that helped many Greeks make the transition to American life was the Greek-language newspaper. The Greek-language press was one of the first non-English presses to develop in the United States. Its popularity was quite remarkable because so few of the early immigrants brought with them the habit of reading newspapers. The newspapers provided an important link between the English- and Greek-speaking worlds. Papers not only contained American news but were also the source of news from Greece. They provided accounts about important events in the villages and provinces, as well as news affecting other Greek American communities in the United States. Almost every Greek American community had its own

Greek Americans relax with favorite old-country activities at a Greek restaurant in New York. Greek immigrants kept their identity alive while making a home in the United States.

newspaper. Because of the newspapers, Greek Americans were able to make greater inroads into the American political, economic, and intellectual life as they taught Greek immigrants about American culture and way of life. The papers too, depending on their point of view, could stir up political rivalries or create new feuds between the different political factions in the Greek American community.

One of the first Greek American newspapers was the *Neos Kosmos* (New World), published in Boston in 1892. Other Greek-language newspapers have included the *Hellenikos Aster* (Greek Star) of Chicago, first printed in 1903 and still published today, but as an English-language newspaper. The *California* of San Francisco, begun in 1907, appeared regularly until the early 1950s, and has since been revived two different times.

While many newspapers came and went, two of the most influential and powerful Greek American newspapers during the early twentieth century were the *Atlantis* and the *National Herald,* whose Greek name was *Ethnikos Kyrix,* both published in New York City. The *Atlantis* first went to press in 1894 as a weekly, but began publishing daily in 1904 and did so continuously until it ceased publication in 1973. The *National Herald,* which began publishing in 1915, offered a perspective different from that of its competitor, the *Atlantis.* When it came to reporting politics for Greek immigrants, the emphasis was on the political happenings in their homeland. The *Atlantis* was the more conservative paper of the two, supporting the Republican Party, while the *National Herald* was identified with liberalism and the Democratic Party.

Although several Greek American English-language newspapers appeared prior to the Second World War, their growth came mainly during the postwar era. Faced with diminishing numbers of Greek newspaper readers, the Greek American press searched for a wider audience among the American born. By the late 1970s, slightly more than half of the Greek press readership read newspapers published exclusively in Eng-

A Different Kind of Newspaper

Besides the large dailies and weeklies in the Greek American press, there also appeared another kind of "newspaper," the kind printed solely for personal reasons, such as attacking or praising certain individuals. Men pretending to be editors would write critical articles about one person. They then would show the articles to enemies of that person, who would pay to have the articles printed as "newspapers." As a rule, these publications did not last very long. Others would print newspapers that covered less important events, describing a local wedding, for example, or the activities of a particular organization. And those unable or unwilling to find a job could always print their own "newspaper."

lish, with about a third reading papers in a bilingual format. Today, only a small minority reads newspapers that are completely in Greek. The leading English-language newspaper is the weekly *Hellenic Chronicle,* which started in 1950. Published in Boston, it specializes in local news and features Greek Americans in public life. Other papers are printed by Greek organizations such as the American Hellenic Education Progressive Association. The Greek Orthodox Church puts out *GOYA* and the bilingual *Orthodox Observer.*

The *Kafenion*

Next to the Greek newspapers, the oldest Greek American institution is the *kafenion,* or coffeehouse, where Greek men met to socialize. The coffeehouse offered a slice of the "old life" and was important for helping many Greek immigrants overcome their homesickness while meeting and talking with other Greeks. As one man described it, "We were very lonely in the United States . . . and the kafenio [coffee house] used to provide us with a place to meet and share our day's experiences, talk about the old country, our families, and, of course, to discuss Greek politics." [34] Along with the church, coffeehouses served as the center of Greek social and cultural life in the United States, particularly during the first years of Greek immigration.

Every Greek community had at least one coffeehouse. Usually some inventive immigrant would rent space in a cheap, convenient location, put in a few tables and chairs, and buy several decks of cards. He would also make sure to have plenty of sweets and

specially brewed coffee such as the kind that Greeks drank at home. There might be a few plants potted in rusty tin cans. The walls might have calendars featuring pictures of pretty women, as well as the Greek and American flags. Maps and pictures of Greece also decorated the walls. With their distinctive Greek names such as Parthenon, Messinia, Arcadia, and Paradisos, the coffeehouses offered a little taste of home and a refuge from work and the stress of living in America.

The coffeehouses were reserved for men. Patrons met their friends there and heard the latest news from home or the local gossip. The coffeehouses were also a good source of information about possible jobs and good places to argue politics. Here men might pick up their mail or entrust the owner with their savings if they were going away on a job. On any given day, men from all walks of life— laborers, shopkeepers, visiting Greek officials and padrones—met to drink coffee, smoke, play the card game called *skampili,* read the newspaper, or discuss current events. Marriages were sometimes arranged in coffeehouses. Some coffeehouses provided various forms of entertainment such as dancers, musicians, and *karagiozi,* or silhouette performers. Others also allowed gambling, which led to police raids, arrests, and, in isolated cases, temporary closings.

The coffeehouses were the subject of frequent criticism from the American public. Many believed that they were centers of trouble and evil goings-on and wanted them closed down permanently. Others simply found them strange and were frightened by the noise and frequent arguments. Periodically the coffeehouses were raided and some patrons arrested. These incidents were often embarrassing because many of the coffeehouse names reflected historical places and events. Local newspapers would carry headlines such as "Parthenon Raided and Seventeen Greeks Arrested" or "The Acropolis Closed,"[35] all of which led to humiliation and ridicule within the Greek immigrant communities.

In time, as many Greek Americans adapted to American life, the coffeehouse lost its appeal and importance. The arrival of Greek women, the growing number of Greek families, and a more comfortable understanding of American ways drew many Greeks away from the coffeehouses. While some still remain in existence, they are not nearly the vital and busy institutions they once were.

Business as Usual

By far the most popular enterprise for many Greek immigrants was the restaurant business. A popular saying among Greeks is that when two Greeks meet, they open a restaurant. Food is important to Greeks and symbolizes friendship and love. To Greeks, failure of a guest to eat is considered to be a great insult to the host and is seen as a rejection of that person's friendship.

Many Greek American restaurateurs got their start because they did not like American food. Remembering the tasty dishes from their homeland, they started cooking for themselves and their neighbors. Often family owned and run, these lunchrooms and restaurants kept long hours and offered low prices and interesting dishes. One of the first recorded mentions of such an enterprise came in the 1880s when a restaurant opened on Roosevelt Street in the lower east side of Manhattan. An American reporter, visiting the establishment later described it as: "a poor, forlorn affair; yet to the lonely immigrant it meant comradeship and a breath of home. . . . Here [the Greeks] found cooking and manners of home."[36] While some establishments served the traditional fare of their homeland, other restaurants expanded their menus, including many American dishes in the hopes of attracting more customers.

Even today, no one knows exactly why Greek immigrants did so well in this tough business. One report published in 1919 offers some insight:

> If the Greek restaurateur succeeded where others failed, it was because he was a better businessman, worked long hours and had imagination and foresight. He used standard, nationally advertised foods, but as a rule did not excel his competitors in the preparation of them. His prices were a trifle lower, but his overhead expenses were about the same. He avoided the establishment of the cabaret eating house, with an orchestra and dancing. . . . This, in essence, was the formula for his success.[37]

Today, many historians consider the Greek Americans' success in the food industry as one of the most interesting phenomena in American business history.

The Church

Along with the coffeehouses and restaurants, the Greek Orthodox Church emerged

St. Mary's in Detroit is home to followers of the Greek Orthodox Church, the major Christian denomination of Greece.

as one of the dominant cultural institutions in the Greek community. Before they were able to establish their own houses of worship, many Greek immigrants visited other churches in the Eastern Orthodox communion, such as a Russian Orthodox church that might be located near their neighborhood. In this way they could still worship according to their traditions. But it was not the same as going to their own churches, where they could hear their own

language and have their own priests. As the number of Greek immigrants increased, many Greek communities took on the task of creating their own Orthodox churches and starting their own parishes, perhaps buying abandoned buildings and recreating the kind of church they had attended back home. Communities that could afford to would build their own churches. The churches became the hub of much activity in the Greek community as they helped new immigrants and more established Greek Americans cope with American life.

The organizing of a Greek parish was very formal. Once a Greek community reached a population of five hundred, a *kinotitos,* or community council was established. The council was headed by a *symvoulion,* or board of directors. Establishing a church was usually the first project of the *kinotitos.* Initially, Greek immigrants wanted their churches to be like the ones that they remembered at home. These churches were often very ornate and sumptuous, with beautiful icons (carved religious statues), and carved screens embellishing the interiors. Many Greek congregations wanted their priests to be like those in the old country and wear ornate robes. Others wished to include in their services a *psaltis,* or male singer, who would lead the choir and congregation in song and prayer.

Congregations often did replicate many of the same features in their churches that they had grown up with in Greece. Greek Orthodox priests, with their long beards, tall hats, and flowing robes, became a common sight in Greek neighborhoods and often stood out in mainstream American cities and towns. The old style of worship was kept intact, too, in Greek American churches, with the men standing on the right side of the church and the women on the left. In time, however, certain practices began disappearing. Pews were introduced into the church so that worshippers could sit, and the service eventually was streamlined. A Greek Orthodox service formerly lasted for hours, for example, but eventually the time was shortened to ninety minutes. Even the priests began changing their appearance:

More and more priests chose to be clean shaven and to wear clothing similar to that of American Catholic priests.

The Greek Orthodox Church in America was not only a place of worship. It was also a place for established residents to meet old friends and for newcomers to become acquainted with the community. With the emergence of a new generation of American-born Greeks, the church took on an additional responsibility with the creation of schools that taught children not only the Greek language but also the history and traditions of Greece. Every day after regular public school had ended, Greek children—some as young as five or six—settled in a vacant store, church basement, or community center to study the Greek language, culture, and history. By the late 1970s, there were approximately four hundred afternoon schools with an enrollment of over thirty thousand students. In addition, the Greek American community established twenty-four day schools, mostly in Chicago and New York, which offered kindergarten through eighth grade classes to a total of sixty-five hundred students. Although many Greek Americans eagerly learned American ways, they still sought to preserve their heritage. As one immigrant noted, it was important to teach "our American-born children . . . the Greek language . . . the Greek character and Greek virtue."[38]

The schools, however, encountered numerous problems. Some Americans misunderstood their purpose and criticized Greeks as "unpatriotic." There was also a shortage of qualified teachers, books, and materials. Children complained that the schools were old-fashioned and that they had to attend not one but two schools. One Greek American man explained why he disliked attending Greek school:

One reason I hated Greek school was because it gave me little time to play or do the things I wanted to do. . . . Imagine a grade school youngster coming home from public school in the late afternoon, then having to ready himself for a school he had no desire to attend . . . taking with him often a chunk of bread or some other edible to curb his appetite, often sitting in bleak, uncomfortable, and sometimes cold surroundings . . . forced to have a late supper, sometimes between 7 and 8 in the evening.[39]

The Greek Orthodox Church emerged as a powerful symbol of the Greek faith and culture in the United States. Both the church and the Greek schools helped immigrants and their families maintain close spiritual and cultural ties with Greece. Even today, the Greek Orthodox Church remains for many Greek Americans the social center of their world.

A Sense of Belonging

Clubs and fraternal organizations were also an important element in the Greek American community. These groups enabled many Greek men and women to forge new friendships, as well as collect money for charities and organize new churches and schools. Most every organization also had unique banners, official seals, and uniforms which identified it.

Often a group, known as a *topika,* or local, had connections with a village or parish in Greece. These organizations were an important force in the Greek community. For example, one son wrote home, "Father, do not feel very badly because of your failure to become mayor . . . for I have

The Atlas Catalog

A familiar sight in many Greek immigrant households was a copy of the Atlas Catalog. Similar to the mail-order catalogs that were published by companies such as Sears Roebuck and Montgomery Ward, the Atlas Catalog was tailored specifically to the Greek immigrant. It listed Greek-English dictionaries, novels translated into Greek, phonographs, records featuring Greek singers and instrumentalists, musical instruments, and sheet music. For prospective brides there were pages of wedding gowns and wedding crowns to be worn by the bride and groom at a Greek Orthodox wedding, candles, invitations, candies, and silver trays. Baptismal gowns and medals for babies could be purchased, as could accessories for coffeehouses such as the *brik* pans used for making strong Turkish coffee and water pipes. Among the best-selling items from the catalog were postcards, which could be bought for a variety of occasions such as birthdays and holidays.

been elected president of our lodge here in America."[40] Clubs were often formed on the basis of regional or village affiliations in which people from common areas could come together. There were also Panhellenic organizations, which were formed to promote Greek heritage and to remind Greek immigrants of their ties to their homeland. The first of these appeared in the years before the First World War. One organization even influenced an estimated forty-two thousand men to return to Greece to defend the country against the Turks in 1912 and 1913.

Some local societies grew to become national organizations and tended to promote one of two viewpoints: maintaining ties with Greece or adaptation to American culture. The American Hellenic Education Progressive Association (AHEPA), founded in Atlanta, Georgia, in 1922, originally provided aid and advice to newly arrived immigrants to help them make the transition to American life. Today, with about 430 chapters nationwide, AHEPA raises money for scholarships for Greek American students and participates in various aid programs in Greece. Founded in 1923, the Greek American Progressive Association, or GAPA, worked to maintain the traditional Greek way of life. Although still active, GAPA's membership is smaller than that of its rival, AHEPA.

Women's organizations also flourished in America. The Daughters of Penelope, an offshoot of AHEPA, founded in 1929 in San Francisco, was organized to unite women of Greek descent. The group today is a leader in philanthropic, educational, and cultural activities with local chapters in the United States, Canada, and Greece. The Daughters of Evrythania, established

Education

In some ways, Greek immigrant children had an easier time adapting to American culture than children from other cultural groups. Many Greek immigrant parents wanted their children to be educated. Because attending school was mandatory in the United States, immigrant children usually received an education, though they were often placed in classes for slow learners because they did not know much English. In many cases, in the Greek home, while Greek was the primary language spoken, it was not uncommon for parents to converse in Greek and have their children answer in English. Not only did the children practice their English, but parents could learn the language too.

In time, the efforts of Greek immigrants to educate themselves and their children paid off, in part because of reforms in education in Greece and the availability of free schooling in the United States. The illiteracy rate for Greek immigrants during the period 1900 to 1908 was 27 percent. By 1910 that figure had dropped to 24 percent, and by 1920, the number of Greek immigrants unable to read or write had decreased to 3.2 percent.

Greek Americans from various clubs in New York celebrate the Greek declaration of independence. Greek American societies and organizations sprang up in many cities.

in Charlotte, North Carolina, focuses more on charitable giving and is also active today. Greek men's and women's organizations also established auxiliaries, or clubs, for young men and women in the Greek community, such as AHEPA's Sons of Per-

icles, Maids of Athens, and the Daughters of Penelope. Intellectual associations that promoted Greek thought and culture were also popular among Greek Americans. The Helicon, organized in Boston in 1911, the Hellenic University Club, established in

1918 in New York City, and the Filiko Society, founded in New York City in 1933, are still in existence. The Filiko Society continues to sponsor public lectures in Greek.

Like the coffeehouses, many of the fraternal organizations that were founded gradually declined as more Greek Americans became more a part of American society. Many children of Greek immigrants rarely joined their parents' organizations, preferring instead to belong to other civic groups, which they believed had more to offer. But the importance of the Greek organizations cannot be underestimated, for they helped many Greeks survive their first years in America.

The Source of Strength and Hope

Another important element in the Greek American community is found closer to home: the family. Greeks are very family-oriented and believe deeply in maintaining close family ties. It was not uncommon for several generations of a family to live under the same roof, or in the same neighborhood. Traditionally, the Greek American family was patriarchal, headed by a father, who supported the family and made most of the decisions.

But while the father or male head of household took care of matters outside the home, the mother was without a doubt the emotional center of the family. Though submissive to her husband, she was the one in charge of the day-to-day goings-on in the house, and it was she who raised and disciplined the children. In many Greek households, a woman who was a *kali nikokira,* or good housekeeper, was clearly more treasured than one who had marketable skills that would allow her to work outside the home.

Greek wives and mothers typically spoke little English; their lives revolved around their family, church, and Greek friends. Quite often these women were widowed early in life, for they often had married men at least a decade older than themselves. Many widows would go to live with their grown children. Despite what might appear to be a limited role in the early Greek communities in the United States, the Greek American women were vital to their success and vitality.

Greek children reflected the roles held by their parents. Boys were clearly favored, while girls were taught to become good wives and housekeepers. Mary Pappas Lines recalled life in her childhood home of five girls and three boys:

> When a brother walked into the room, our mother would say, annoyed at our remaining seated, "Get up and give your brother your chair." If the family was going out to a church function or some kind of gathering and one or the other of our brothers hadn't come home, one of us sisters had to stay behind to heat the food and serve him. [41]

Discipline was strictly enforced in the Greek household, as many parents believed that a good parent needed to use hard punishment to raise a successful child.

Along with their families, the Greek immigrants succeeded in transplanting many of the institutions that were familiar to them back home. All of these helped the Greek immigrant community to grow and acclimate to American society, while offering some respite from much that was unfamiliar and frightening. Some new institutions, such as the opening of Greek restaurants, helped the immigrants become more a part of the American community at large. Other institutions, such as the Greek Orthodox Church, would weather change among the Greek immigrant community, while fraternal clubs and coffeehouses would decrease in importance and influence as Greek immigrants became more comfortable with America.

CHAPTER SEVEN

Trying to Fit

Like other immigrant groups who came to America, the Greeks encountered more than their share of hostility and resentment. Many Americans did not want Greeks in the country. Some believed that Greeks and their culture were too strange and would never fit into American society. Others thought Greeks might be dangerous and subversive, or a threat to the government and national security. This intense fear of the Greeks and other immigrants has a name: xenophobia. Ironically, the English word is based on the Greek words for "strangers" and "fear."

Thus it was that Greek immigrants soon realized that besides having to conquer a new language, acquire new customs, and learn a new way of life, they would have to battle discrimination. In many cases, the Greeks prevailed in asserting themselves as members of American society. But it was not always easy, and some people paid with their lives.

No Greeks Apply

A rude surprise awaited many Greeks arriving in America, as native-born Americans did little to make them welcome. One immigrant remembered his first months in America as "an agonizing time; we were beat up just for being Greek."[42] Some Greeks recall how people would shout and curse at them or make fun of their accents. An observer of Greek immigrant life in Lowell, Massachusetts, noted that the "average American citizen" thought of the newly arrived Greek immigrants as a "quarrelsome, treacherous, filthy, low-living lot."[43] Greek children were not immune from bigotry either; growing up in the immigrant neighborhoods near the factories and mills, they were often picked on by the children of other immigrant groups. Greek immigrant Sam Fortosis described his experience as a young Greek immigrant growing up in New York:

If you were Greek or Italian you were considered low class, very low class, because you couldn't speak English. And

Standing on a New York sidewalk, an immigrant girl carries an unfinished coat. Greek children were often bullied by the children of other immigrant groups.

[the Americans] didn't know anything about the Greeks. We weren't welcome over here. If you weren't strong enough to fight, you just got a lickin'. . . . But when we could speak a few words of English . . . we started giving it back. [44]

Many Greek immigrants applying for jobs found that a number of establishments refused to hire them simply because of their nationality. One immigrant who applied for a waiter's job in a New York restaurant was flatly turned down. As he recalled the encounter, he said, "The boss would say, 'What are you?' When I said, 'Greek,' he would answer, 'There's no job.'" [45] Even restaurant advertisements left little doubt about how some establishments felt toward the new arrivals. As a result of ads like "John's Restaurant, Pure American, No Rats, No Greeks," [46] many Greeks depended on other Greeks who had started their own businesses to help them find jobs.

No Place to Fit

In their relations with other immigrants, the Greeks faced problems too. Older, more established immigrant groups such as the Irish and the Germans resented the Greeks for coming to America. Jobs were an especially contentious issue. Greeks were accused of taking factory jobs for lower wages than local workers were obtaining, and other immigrants thought nothing of attacking and intimidating Greek workers. In some cases, Greek immigrants unknowingly brought unwelcome attention to themselves by acting as strikebreakers in factories and mills where workers were picketing for better wages and working conditions. Looking only for work, and not understanding the role of labor unions, Greeks often took the jobs of striking workers, thus increasing the already high tensions among Greeks, other immigrants, and native-born Americans.

The early years of the twentieth century were often marked by such incidents. In

A Religion Recognized

One other sign that the Greek American community was now fully established within American society came in the late 1950s, when the Greek Orthodox Church was formally recognized as a major faith in the United States by twenty-six state legislatures. By this time, Greek Orthodox churches had grown to number almost 250 throughout the country. In 1957, Archbishop Michael, the head of the Greek Orthodox Church in America, became the first Greek Orthodox hierarch to participate in a presidential inauguration ceremony, as Dwight D. Eisenhower took the oath of office for the second time. And in another show of recognition, the U.S. Department of Defense agreed to authorize an Eastern Orthodox dogtag for Greek American servicemen. The move meant that Greek American GIs no longer would have their religion described as "other" on their identification tags.

1904, in Chicago, a strike had broken out in a number of diesel shops in the city. Many workers in other diesel shops left their jobs in support of the strike. A group of inexperienced and newly arrived Greeks filled these jobs, drawing criticism not only from labor leaders and the striking workers, but from Greek businessmen, fearful that the anti-Greek hostility would hurt them as well. Community leaders and Greek organizations united and made a plea to the workers and other Greeks in the community: "Our neighbors who are working as we are belong to unions and they are fighting for higher wages to improve the standard of living of the working class. By taking their jobs when they strike, we commit an offense at them and ourselves. . . . Let us be part of this land of plenty and not remain predatory aliens."[47]

Greeks in the many mill and factory towns of New England faced physical violence from the community. As the third major immigrant group coming to the region, after the French Canadians and the Irish, the Greeks posed a serious threat to job security, especially to the other immigrant groups. Not only did they work for less money, but the Greeks soon earned a reputation for being more reliable and consistent workers, unlike the Irish and French Canadians, who were stereotyped as having a tendency to drink and cause trouble. One early account described the situation:

> From the very beginning these two dominant races [the Irish and the French Canadians] attacked and ill-used the new Greek laborers and hounded them from good lodgings.

Their attacks grew as the Greek colony grew. At night when the mills poured out their operatives [workers], the poor, scared Greeks would gather twenty or so together in the middle of the street, scatter to their lodgings and dare not stir out till morning.[48]

A Hostile Land

It seemed that no matter where they settled, Greek immigrants might find themselves the targets of hostility. While Greeks experienced discrimination and hostility in the northeastern and midwestern United States, it was in the West that they encountered the most bitter reaction and the most serious incidents. This was due in part to the growing number of Greek immigrants who were settling and working in the West, thus becoming more visible in their new communities.

For instance, in 1908, three Greek immigrants were killed in an antiforeigner clash in Nevada. The neighboring state of Utah was the scene of many hostile incidents as well. There, Greeks were the target of escalating hostilities with the Mormons, and with other state residents. Many Greeks believed that the attacks were due to their growing success in business, which many American businessmen and shop owners found threatening. In 1917 a Greek accused of murdering the brother of heavyweight champion boxer Jack Dempsey was almost lynched by an angry Utah mob. Elsewhere throughout the state, local citizens broke into and vandalized Greek businesses; the Ku Klux Klan, which was particularly active in the Utah area, targeted Greek immigrants too.

Fighting for Freedom

To help the Greeks in their struggle against the Nazis, the U.S. Army created the 122nd Infantry Battalion in 1943. Composed of both Greek Americans and Greek nationals, the battalion's goal was to invade and help liberate Greece. The battalion had two mottos: "Liberty or death," from the American patriot Patrick Henry during the American Revolution, and "One day of freedom than forty years a slave," which was used by Greek revolutionaries in their war for independence from Turkey in 1821. The "122" used to identify the battalion also had special significance: It represented the number of years that had passed since the 1821 revolt. Included in the battalion were three hundred parachute troops who were dropped into Greece to dynamite and destroy strategic bridges and roads.

The most publicized of these anti-Greek incidents took place in South Omaha, Nebraska, in 1909. At that time, several thousand Greek laborers were living in a shantytown just outside the city. Tensions against the Greeks were already high; many locals believed that the Greeks, unlike their well-behaved compatriots in New England, spent too much time carousing and gambling. People also viewed the immigrants as strikebreakers, adding to the already tense atmosphere. On February 19, a Greek man, John Masourides, who was walking with an American woman thought to be a prostitute, was stopped by a policeman. Words were exchanged and Masourides killed the policeman, whom the Greeks later accused of having been drunk and angry at seeing a Greek walking with a "white" woman. Masourides claimed he had killed the policeman in self-defense, but the people of South Omaha were not in a mood to listen. In retaliation, a mob stormed the Greek business quarter and burned most of it to the ground. Thirty-six businesses were lost, many of the Greeks fled the city. The incident received national and international coverage and even prompted the Greek government to demand that the victims of the mob violence be compensated with $135,000. Not until 1918 did the U.S. government respond, but payments to the victims of the incident amounted to only $40,000.

Becoming American

While battling negative attitudes and stereotypes about their culture, Greek immigrants worked hard to assimilate within mainstream American society. Perhaps ironically, one helpful factor was the passage of laws that restricted immigration and set limits on how many people could come from a particular country. For instance, between 1922 and 1924, the number of Greeks allowed to come into the United States was set at one hundred a year, whereas in 1921, twenty-eight thousand Greeks entered the country, as well as tens of thousands from other lands.

Because of the new restrictions, many Greek immigrants now sought to become citizens to make it easier for their relatives to join them. It was legal for a naturalized citizen to bring family members living in a foreign country to the United States. The impact this law had on the Greek community was dramatic: In 1920 one out of six Greeks sought citizenship, but by 1930 three out every six Greeks were applying to become citizens. In time, too, the first generation of Greek Americans would be replaced by their children, Greek Americans who were born in the United States, thereby rooting the Greek American community to its adopted country even more deeply. The increase of Greek immigrant women coming to America also helped the Greek American community flourish and become even more settled as Greek neighborhoods were filled with the sounds of families and children.

Many Greek Americans enjoyed financial success in the United States through a variety of businesses and services. But with the onset of the Great Depression, during the 1930s, they, along with thousands of other Americans, were hit hard economically. Many lost their businesses; others limped along, hoping to ride the difficult time. The depression and the repeal of Prohibition in 1933 offered one new business opportunity, however, as many Greeks entered the bar and package liquor business. Still, some Greeks had had enough, and for the only time in history, the number of Greeks returning to their homeland exceeded the number coming to America.

The period also saw a shift in political loyalties on two fronts. Prior to the depression, the majority of Greek Americans tended to pay closer attention to the politics of their homeland. Bitter feuds and rivalries had been stirred up over the years between those who supported the monarchy and those loyal to the faction that had forced King Constantine to give up his throne in 1917. As these political feuds began dying out, the Greek American community in turn was becoming more unified and strong.

If Greek Americans were less concerned with Greek politics, they were becoming increasingly attentive to the U.S. political scene. Initially, many Greeks were strong supporters of the Republican Party with its strong emphasis on business and its more conservative political platform. But by the 1930s, Greek Americans were supporting President Franklin D. Roosevelt, the Democratic Party, and the New Deal programs, and would continue to back the Democrats in the future. And unlike many other immigrant groups who supported socialism, Greek Americans tended to stay away from radical causes and groups. This was due in part to the reluctance of the Greek immigrants to commit themselves to groups or issues that were deemed "unpatriotic" to the American way of life. Also, for many Greeks, there simply was not enough time, nor did they have the energy, to support such groups. Some, perhaps most, were trying to make their businesses succeed, while others were more concerned about earning enough money to return to Greece.

Greek Americans at War

The outbreak of the Second World War helped Greek Americans assimilate even further. Many Greeks watched and listened anxiously to the news that their home country had been invaded by Italy in 1940. The initial successes of the Greek army in holding off the invaders made headlines throughout the United States, giving the Greek American community a great deal of exposure, while highlighting Greek pride at their countrymen's struggles. Efforts were also undertaken to provide war relief, and the Greek War Relief Association (GWRA) raised over $5 million in money and supplies. When the Nazis invaded and later occupied Greece, the GWRA continued its efforts, sending seven-hundred thousand tons of food, clothing, and medicine to Greece.

Still, some Greek Americans worried that their homeland might, in the end, join the Nazi's side, known as the Axis; such a move would jeopardize the Greek Americans' status as patriotic U.S. citizens.

A Nazi convoy overtakes a group of Greek peasants. Greek Americans sent provisions to help their homeland during the Second World War.

Greek soldiers capture a guerrilla sniper on the Albanian frontier.

Therefore, when the United States entered the war in 1941, Greek American support for the Allies was wholehearted. Thousands of Greek Americans rushed to join the American military to show their support and patriotism. At home, Greek Americans bought and sold war bonds, which funneled money into the American war effort. One Greek American, Michael Loris, was named champion U.S. war bond salesman in 1942 for selling 24,142 war bonds.

Postwar Prosperity and Security

In the years following the war, the Greek American community had become more firmly entrenched in mainstream American society. A good number of Greek Americans, through hard work and diligence, had risen to become part of the American mid-dle class. The community was dominated by small businessmen, another sign of the Greek entrepreneurial spirit that had helped so many during their early years in America. Gone were pushcarts and outdoor stands. Many Greeks now owned storefront businesses, and many had become very successful in their fields. While a small mi-

Greece in 1942

Belles and Baseball

During the Second World War, Greek American women, like many other women, found themselves stepping in to take the place of men who were away fighting the war. Many found work in grocery stores and restaurants, or went to work at one of the many factories manufacturing items for the war effort. Some younger Greek American women broke with Greek tradition in a more dramatic way: playing baseball. When Chicago Cubs owner Philip Wrigley began his nationwide talent search in 1942 to form a women's professional baseball league, the daughters of Greek immigrants could be found on the roster. Among the Greek American players in the league were Kay Lionikis, who played third base for the Springfield (Illinois) Sallies, and Anastasia Batikis, an outfielder for the Racine (Wisconsin) Belles. This break with traditional women's roles signaled the growing independence of the younger Greek American generation, especially the women, in determining their own destiny.

nority of the Greek American community still struggled in poverty, overall Greek Americans had forged for themselves a path to economic security and acceptance in American society.

The postwar period also saw a transition of sorts among many of the long-standing Greek organizations in the country. As more Greeks became citizens and joined mainstream American society, the older, more tradition-based immigration societies, founded during the first wave of Greek immigration, gradually began disappearing. Other organizations such as AHEPA, which encouraged Greeks to become more "Americanized," continued to grow and thrive, meeting new challenges facing the Greek American community. Along with the Greek Orthodox Church, these organizations in the coming years would provide direction and guidance not only to new immigrants arriving in the United States, but to the established Greek Americans.

EPILOGUE

Greek and American

Today, as in the nineteenth century, Greek Americans play an important role in the American melting pot. Many Greek Americans continue to honor their heritage both in their everyday lives and in the numerous Greek festivals and celebrations in American cities large and small. Even though the number of Greek immigrants to this country has declined considerably, averaging fewer than twenty-five hundred persons a year, Greek culture remains strong and vibrant.

Even so, Greek Americans have encountered difficulties. Up until the Second World War, the Greek American community was made up of two main groups: the first generation of immigrants, who came to America from Europe, and the second generation, most of whom had been born in the United States. During the postwar years, the Greek American community became more mixed, as immigrants not only from Greece and Turkey, but also from Cyprus and other areas of the world where Greeks lived, arrived in America. While this meant a fresh influx of Greek culture and tradition, the newcomers' attitudes sometimes clashed with those of Greek Americans who now saw themselves as more American than Greek.

Greektowns

A visit to one of the many "Greektowns" in the United States today illustrates how old and new traditions have come together, sometimes harmoniously, sometimes not. One is likely to be overwhelmed with the dizzying array of shops, stores, and businesses. Restaurants, produce stands, grocery stores, fish stores, bakeries, and sweet shops are just a few places where one can stop to savor some of the favorite dishes of Greek Americans. There are also souvenir shops and newsstands, which carry Greek American newspapers as well as Greek newspapers and magazines. These neighborhoods are still home to many Greek social clubs, Greek travel agencies, and Greek Orthodox funeral parlors. Where once these neighborhood businesses catered mainly to local residents, today many people, both Greek and non-Greek from outside the neighborhood, make a point of visiting.

In some respects, the neighborhoods in Greektowns have changed little. For many, the preferred housing is a two- or three-story house, known as a double-decker or

This photograph shows a restaurant in Chicago's Greektown. Greek Americans keep traditions alive in Greektowns across the country.

triple-decker, with the owner occupying the ground floor level and the upper stories rented out, usually to other Greeks. In the evenings, some of the men of the neighborhood might be seen wandering into a social club for an evening of visiting, drinking coffee, and playing cards. While in recent years, neighborhoods have had to deal with crime such as Greek youth gangs, residents continue to work hard at keeping their streets and homes safe.

But these neighborhoods are changing. Now more non-Greeks are moving into the areas, while many Greeks are leaving the old neighborhoods to live in homes farther away. Those who have done well financially are usually the first to leave. But many believe that as long as there is a continued supply of "new blood" in the form of newly arrived immigrants from Greece, the Greektowns will thrive and maintain many of the old ways and traditions of Greece.

The Church: Progress or Past

The presence of the Greek Orthodox Church remains strong in Greek American communities and reflects many of the tensions that Greek Americans are grappling with today. One of the greatest concerns among church leaders and older, more traditional Greek Americans has been the lack of interest in Hellenism, or the history and culture of Greece. There is a feeling among the more recent generations of Greek Americans that Hellenism is outdated and old-fashioned and has no place in modern Greek American life. Attendance at Greek schools is down: Whereas children once attended Greek

school every day, now it is more common to go once or twice a week, if at all. As a result, there is now a younger Greek American generation with little or no knowledge of Greek language, history, and culture.

In recent years the church has tried in a number of ways to reach the younger generation. For instance, in 1970 the Greek Orthodox Church approved the substitution of English for Greek in its services. While many among the older generations were dismayed by the change, others viewed it as the most realistic action the church could take to remain an important and relevant institution among Greek Americans, many of whom are not familiar with the Greek language.

The church has also grappled with the decision over whether to separate itself from the Orthodox Eastern Church in Istanbul, much as the American Russian Orthodox Church did from the mother church in Moscow in 1970. Such a move would make the Greek Orthodox Church an autonomous institution, standing alone and creating its own policies and doctrines, which many younger members would prefer. However there are those who have argued against such a move, seeing it as a "disowning" of the church's important traditions and its past.

Another new development within the Greek Orthodox Church has been the growing number of non-Greeks in the congregations. The majority of these persons come to the church through intermarriage with a Greek American. Although once it was undesirable to take a non-Greek as a spouse, today, attitudes toward the practice are changing. So are the numbers: In 1926 it

The Importance of Tradition

Many Greek Americans continue to celebrate traditional Greek holidays and customs. For example, they bring a baby to church forty days after birth to be blessed, and they have the child christened within a year after that. When a Greek American dies, a wake is held immediately, with the funeral the following day. Easter continues to be the most important church holiday celebrated, followed by Christmas. On Holy Apostles' Day, June 29, the people honor Saints Peter and Paul.

Greek Americans also celebrate special holidays, such as Greek Independence Day on March 25, with parades in traditional costumes, speeches, and folk dances. Another secular holiday celebrated by Greek Americans is "No" Day, October 28, which commemorates the refusal of the Greek government to give in to the fascists during the Second World War.

was estimated that one in five Greeks married a non-Greek. During the 1960s, however, mixed couples accounted for three out of ten church marriages. By the 1970s the number had increased to five out of ten. Even non-Greeks have played important roles in the church, sitting on committees and being active in church functions. Their presence in the parishes will continue to have a profound influence on the direction of the Greek American church in years to come.

The growing incidence of Greeks marrying non-Greeks has also raised concerns that such marriages will gradually erode Greek culture and heritage, threatening the very nature of the Greek family. Respect for marriage between Greeks remains strong, and even though more Greeks are marrying people from other cultures and nations, for most Greeks, marrying another Greek is still very important.

The presence of non-Greek church members at Greek Orthodox Church services, and the participation of non-Greeks in the Greek American community, are just a few of the changes now taking place. Whereas once several generations of a family lived together under one roof, many of today's Greek American families are not as close and are more likely to live as nuclear family units, separated from older relatives and other family members. Growing numbers of elderly Greek Americans are admitted to nursing homes rather than being cared for at home. Attendance in Greek schools is declining rapidly, as third- and fourth-generation Greek American children resent spending their afternoons learning a language and traditions that seem irrelevant to them. For many of today's young Greek Americans, contact with older members of the Greek American community is fading, occurring only at church and certain social functions.

The issue of education in general continues to concern Greek Americans. While levels of education are up for Greek Americans, they still lag behind other immigrant groups

Singing the *Rebitka*

One of the fastest growing businesses in the last several years in Greek American communities has been the Greek nightclub. Featuring musical acts from Greece, the clubs have become very popular among Greek Americans and non-Greeks too. In addition to contemporary and popular music of Greece, the clubs offer traditional singing and dancing. One specialty consists of acts that feature the *rebitka*, a unique musical sound that has been compared with American jazz and blues. *Rebitkas* were songs that described the poverty and despair of Greek life. The songs also told of overcoming one's troubles or, as one Greek immigrant described in Helen Papanikolas's book, *An Amulet of Greek Earth*, "the man who had a sorrow and threw it out." But the *rebitka* was not always so popular. For many years, educated and middle-class Greeks saw the music and its musicians and singers as a form of lower-class entertainment.

as one of the least formally educated groups in the United States. Still, Greek Americans on average enjoy an income that is 10 percent higher than all other groups, and their rate of unemployment is much lower. Few Greek Americans live below the poverty line or are on welfare. As Greek Americans become better educated, they are entering skilled professions that pay higher wages.

Greek Contributions

In the process of becoming more a part of the American mainstream, Greek Americans have made many invaluable contributions to American society in such areas as the arts, politics, business, and science. Among Greek Americans who have contributed to American culture are opera diva Maria Callas and prima ballerina Helen Alexopoulos. Noted artists Theodore Stamos, William Baziotes, and Peter Voulkas are all of Greek American heritage.

In the world of stage and film some of the most noted Greek Americans are Academy Award–winning director Elia Kazan and actor-director John Cassavetes. Actors such as Telly Savalas, John Stamos, and Billy Zane have demonstrated their talents in film and television. Two popular newcomers to television are Greek American: Melina Kanakaredes and Paula Korologos Cale. Olympia Dukakis, Oscar-winning actress, is also the cousin of another notable Greek American: former Massachusetts governor and 1988 Democratic presidential candidate Michael Dukakis. Other noted Greek Americans in the field of entertainment include film critic Andrew Sarris, CBS news reporter Ike Pappas, and Anthony D. Thomopoulos, who served as president of the Entertainment Division of ABC.

The field of politics has attracted a number of other Greek Americans, including former Maryland governor Spiro T. Agnew, who was vice president under Richard M.

Nixon until 1973, when he was forced to resign because evidence surfaced of political corruption during his years in Maryland. In 1978, at age thirty-seven, Paul Tsongas of Massachusetts became the youngest-ever member of the U.S. Senate. And also in 1978, Olympia Bouchles Snow of Maine became the youngest-ever woman to be elected to the House of Representatives; she was thirty-one. Snow was also the first-ever Greek American woman in the House.

Other prominent Greek Americans in the arena of politics and government are former presidential adviser George Stephanopoulos, who upon leaving the administration of Bill Clinton went on to become a political analyst and commentator. Author Arianna Huffington has also emerged as one of the leading voices of the American conservative political movement. They, along with other Greek American elected officials demonstrate the growing political presence and influence of the Greek American community today.

Former presidential adviser George Stephanopoulos marries Alexandra Wentworth at the Holy Trinity Cathedral Greek Orthodox Church in New York.

Babe Didrikson, an Olympic golfer, married George Zaharis, a Greek American wrestler. After their marriage in 1939, he became her manager and advisor.

The field of sports has seen many talented Greek American athletes including former football player Alex Karras, sportscaster Bob Costas, and tennis champion Pete Sampras. The owner of the Baltimore Orioles baseball team is Greek American Peter Angelos. Prominent Greek American baseball players have included Gus Niarchaos, Milt Pappas, and Gus Traindos. Detroit Red Wings hockey player Christos Chelios was born and raised in a Greek American neighborhood in Chicago. Winning Olympic medals for the United States were Greek American decathlon star Bob Mathias and diver Greg Louganis. Many sports fans have taken the advice of another well-known Greek American: Las Vegas odds maker and gambler Jimmy "the Greek" Snyder, who was born James Synadinos.

Greek Americans who have made significant contributions to the worlds of science and industry include Dr. George Nicholas Papanicolaou, inventor of the so-called Pap test, used to detect cervical and uterine cancers, and Spyros P. Skouras, Hollywood movie mogul. Skouras began a chain of movie theaters, initiated Cinemascope technology, and eventually became the president of 20th Century Fox Film Corporation. Skouras was the first owner to allow African Americans into his theaters in Missouri, and he never permitted racial or ethnic slurs in any film he financed. Other Greek Americans who have made a mark in the business world include William Tavoulareas, who headed Mobil Oil, and Louis Anderson, the general manager of the Onassis shipping organization.

Challenges to the Community

In spite of their many contributions to American life and culture, the Greek American community in the United States faces ongoing challenges. For many Greek Americans, for example, the need to balance their Greek and American heritages is ever present. Even today, arguments and some divisiveness within the Greek community have arisen over the issue of assimilation, especially between the newcomers and old-timers.

For Greek Americans today, the task ahead is how to best incorporate the institutions brought to the United States more than a century ago into their twenty-first-century communities. As long as new Greek immigrants come to America, many of those institutions and attitudes will remain intact. Like any other ethnic group, the Greeks' greatest challenge is in demonstrating their sense of pride in their country of origin, while remembering and honoring those who came before and made the Greek American immigrant experience such a successful one.

Notes

Introduction: The Greek Odyssey

1. Quoted in David M. Brownstone, Irene M. Franck, and Douglass Brownstone, *Island of Hope, Island of Tears*. New York: Barnes & Noble Books, 2000, p. 72.

Chapter One: A Country Full of Woe

2. Theodore Saloutos, *The Greeks in the United States*. Cambridge, MA: Harvard University Press, 1964, p. 3.
3. Quoted in Gladys Nadler Rips, *Coming to America: Immigrants from Southern Europe*. New York: Delacorte Press, 1981, pp. 63–64.
4. Saloutos, *The Greeks in the United States*, p. 7.
5. Quoted in Saloutos, *The Greeks in the United States*, p. 30.
6. Quoted in Helen Papanikolas, *An Amulet of Greek Earth: Generations of Immigrant Folk Culture*. Athens, OH: Swallow Press, 2002, p. 175.
7. Quoted in Rips, *Coming to America*, p. 69.

Chapter Two: "Mother, I Want to Go to Foreign Lands"

8. Quoted in Brownstone, Franck, and Brownstone, *Island of Hope, Island of Tears*, p. 47.
9. Quoted in Charles Moskos, *Greek Americans: Struggle and Success*, 2nd ed. New Brunswick, NJ: Transaction Press, 1990, p. 8.
10. Quoted in Theodore Saloutos, *They Remember America: The Story of the Repatriated Greek-Americans*. Berkeley: University of California Press, 1956, p. 3.
11. Quoted in Leola Benedict Thurhune, "The Greek Bootblack," *Survey* September 16, 1911, pp. 853–54.

Chapter Three: Coming to America

12. Quoted Papanikolas, *An Amulet of Greek Earth*, p. 53.
13. Quoted in Mary Shapiro, *Gateway to Liberty: The Story of the Statue of Liberty and Ellis Island*. New York: Vintage Books, 1986, p. 102.
14. Quoted in Wilton S. Tifft, *Ellis Island*. Chicago: Contemporary Books, 1989, p. 86.
15. Quoted in Saloutos, *They Remember America*, p. 3.
16. Quoted in Shapiro, *Gateway to Liberty*, p. 92.
17. Quoted in Rips, *Coming to America*, p. 72.

Chapter Four: Ellis Island

18. Quoted in Brownstone, Franck, and Brownstone, *Island of Hope, Island of Tears*, p. 141.
19. Quoted in Tifft, *Ellis Island*, p. 33.
20. Quoted in Shapiro, *Gateway to Liberty*, p. 162.
21. Quoted in Shapiro, *Gateway to Liberty*, p. 163.
22. Quoted in Brownstone, Franck, and Brownstone, *Island of Hope, Island of Tears*, pp. 162–63.
23. Quoted in Shapiro, *Gateway to Liberty*, p. 167.

24. Quoted in Brownstone, Franck, and Brownstone, *Island of Hope, Island of Tears,* p. 165.

25. Quoted in Tifft, *Ellis Island,* p. 33.

Chapter Five: Earning a Living

26. Quoted in Saloutos, *The Greeks in the United States,* p. 46.

27. Quoted in Gunther Peck, *Reinventing Free Labor: Padrones and Immigrant Workers in the North American West, 1880–1930.* New York: Cambridge University Press, 2000, p. 203.

28. Quoted in Thurhune, "The Greek Bootblack."

29. Quoted in Saloutos, *The Greeks in the United States,* p. 55.

30. Quoted in Moskos, *Greek Americans,* p. 15.

31. Quoted in Papanikolas, *An Amulet of Greek Earth,* p. 124.

32. Quoted in Papanikolas, *An Amulet of Greek Earth,* p. 135.

Chapter Six: Living Greek, Becoming American

33. Quoted in Saloutos, *The Greeks in the United States,* pp. 88–89.

34. Quoted in Alice Scourby, *The Greek Immigrants.* Boston: Twayne, 1984, p. 29.

35. Quoted in Saloutos, *The Greeks in the United States,* p. 82.

36. Quoted in Moskos, *Greek Americans,* p. 123.

37. Quoted in Saloutos, *The Greeks in the United States,* p. 268.

38. Quoted in Saloutos, *The Greeks in the United States,* p. 100.

39. Quoted in Papanikolas, *An Amulet of Greek Earth,* p. 195.

40. Quoted in Saloutos, *The Greeks in the United States,* p. 106.

41. Quoted in Papanikolas, *An Amulet of Greek Earth,* p. 199.

Chapter Seven: Trying to Fit

42. Quoted in Scourby, *The Greek Immigrants,* p. 28.

43. Moskos, *Greek Americans,* p. 18.

44. Quoted in Rips, *Coming to America,* p. 83.

45. Quoted in Scourby, *The Greek Immigrants,* p. 28.

46. Quoted in Scourby, *The Greek Immigrants,* p. 47.

47. Quoted in Saloutos, *The Greeks in the United States,* p. 62.

48. Quoted in Moskos, *Greek Americans,* p. 18.

FOR FURTHER READING

Periodicals

Cobblestone Magazine, "Greek Americans," December 1996. This entire issue is devoted to the history and culture of Greek Americans.

Books

Jayne Jones, *The Greeks in America.* Minneapolis, MN: Lerner Publications, 1990. An overview of the history and culture of Greek Americans.

Dimitris Monos, *The Greek Americans.* New York: Chelsea House, 1988. A history of Greeks in the United States.

Marilyn Rouvelas, *A Guide to Greek Traditions and Customs in America.* Betheseda, MD: Attica Press, 1993. A guide to the many religious and nonreligious traditions that Greek Americans observe and celebrate.

Conrad R. Stein, *Ellis Island.* Chicago: Childrens Press, 1992. A brief history of Ellis Island.

Books

David M. Brownstone, Irene M. Franck, and Douglass Brownstone, *Island of Hope, Island of Tears.* New York: Barnes & Noble Books, 2000. First-person accounts of immigrant experiences at Ellis Island and in America.

Thomas Burgess, *Greeks in America: An Account of Their Coming, Progress, Customs, Living and Aspirations.* Boston: Sherman, French & Company, 1913. An early history of Greek immigrants in the United States.

Richard Clogg, *A Short History of Modern Greece.* London: Cambridge University Press, 1979. A historical overview of Greece from 1204 to 1979.

Roger Daniels, *Coming to America: A History of Immigration and Ethnicity in American Life.* New York: HarperCollins, 1990. A broad overview chronicling the history of American immigration.

David Holden, *Greece Without Columns.* Philadelphia: J.B. Lippincott, 1972. A comprehensive history of modern Greece.

Melvin G. Holli and Peter d'A. Jones, *Ethnic Chicago.* Grand Rapids, MI: William B. Eerdmans, 1984. Includes a chapter on Greek Americans in Chicago.

George A. Kourvetaris, *Studies on Greek Americans.* New York: Columbia University Press, 1997. A collection of essays discussing the Greek immigrant experience.

William C. McGrew, *Land and Revolution in Modern Greece, 1800–1881.* Antioch, OH: Kent State University Press, 1985.

The struggle over land and land reform is the subject of this book.

Charles Moskos, *Greek Americans: Struggle and Success,* 2nd ed. New Brunswick, NJ: Transaction Press, 1990. A thorough history of the Greek immigrant experience in the United States.

Ann Novotny, *Strangers at the Door: Ellis Island, Castle Garden and the Great Migration to America.* Riverside, CT: Chatham Press, 1971. A good history of Ellis Island with numerous firsthand accounts.

Helen Papanikolas, *An Amulet of Greek Earth: Generations of Immigrant Folk Culture.* Athens, OH: Swallow Press, 2002. A study of Greek culture in the United States.

Gunther Peck, *Reinventing Free Labor: Padrones and Immigrant Workers in the North American West, 1880–1930.* New York: Cambridge University Press, 2000. An in-depth study of the padrone system.

Gladys Nadler Rips, *Coming to America: Immigrants from Southern Europe.* New York: Delacorte Press, 1981. Among the immigrant groups covered in this book are the Greeks.

Theodore Saloutos, *The Greeks In the United States.* Cambridge, MA: Harvard University Press, 1964. One of the first books by a Greek American to present an in-depth look at the Greek immigrants.

———, "Greeks." In *Harvard Encyclopedia of American Ethnic Groups.* Cambridge, MA: Harvard University Press, 1980, pp. 430–40.

———, *They Remember America: The Story of the Repatriated Greek-Americans.* Berkeley: University of California Press,

1956. First-person accounts of Greek immigrants and their experiences in America.

Alice Scourby, *The Greek Immigrants*. Boston: Twayne, 1984. An overview of the Greek immigrants, particularly good on family and social institutions.

Mary Shapiro, *Gateway to Liberty: The Story of the Statue of Liberty and Ellis Island*. New York: Vintage Books, 1986. The sections on Ellis Island provide a history of the institution and include many first-person accounts.

Wilton S. Tifft, *Ellis Island*. Chicago: Contemporary Books, 1989. A history of Ellis Island; included are first-person accounts of immigrants who came through there.

Virginia Yans-McLaughlin and Marjorie Lightman, with the Statue of Liberty-Ellis Island Foundation, *Ellis Island and the Peopling of America: The Official Guide*. New York: The New Press, 1990. A history and resource guide of Ellis Island.

Periodicals

Dan Georgakas, "The Greeks in America," *Journal of the Hellenic Diaspora*, vol. 14, nos. 1–2, 1987.

"Life Story of a Pushcart Peddlar," *Independent*, vol. 60, 1960.

Victor S. Papacosma, "The Greek Press in America," *Journal of the Hellenic Diaspora*, vol. 5, no. 4, 1979.

Theodore Saloutos, "Causes and Patterns of Greek Emigration to the United States," *Perspectives in American History*, vol. 7, 1973.

Leola Benedict Thurhune, "The Greek Bootblack," *Survey*, September 16, 1911.

Websites

Utah's Greek Americans (www.kued.org). An overview of the history of Greek immigrants in Utah.

Immigration to Acclimation (www.hellenicmuseum.org). This online exhibit from the Hellenic Museum in Chicago provides a history of Greek immigrants in the United States, particularly those who came to Chicago.

Acropolis of America: The Greek Community of Lowell (www.ecommunity.uml.edu). A history of the Greeks who settled in Lowell, Massachusetts.

INDEX

PICTURE CREDITS

Cover Photo: © Getty Images
© Bettmann/CORBIS, 11, 48, 55, 58, 67, 75
© CORBIS, 18, 42, 51
© Kevin Fleming/CORBIS, 71
© Robert Holmes/CORBIS, 89
© Eric and David Hosking/CORBIS, 15
© Hulton/Archive, 17, 24, 27, 31, 34, 45,
   46, 79, 86

© Christie's Images/CORBIS, 39
© Michael Maslam Historic
   Photographs/CORBIS, 63
© Reuters NewMedia Inc./CORBIS, 93
PhotoDisk, 13
© Underwood & Underwood/CORBIS,
   94
Steve Zmina, 16, 22, 37

About the Author

Meg Greene is a writer and historian with degrees in history and historic preservation. She is the author of fifteen books and numerous articles. Two of her books have won awards: *Slave Young, Slave Long* was recognized as a 1999 Honor Book from the Society of School Librarians International for grades 7–12, and *Buttons, Bones, and the Organ Grinder's Monkey* was chosen as a 2001 New York Public Library Best Book for Teens. She is also a contributing editor to "History for Children," for Suite 101.com. Ms. Greene makes her home in Virginia.